A Cat and Dog Look at the Cross

A CAT AND DOG LOOK AT THE CROSS

Bob Sjogren and Kevin Kimbrough

Transforming lives through God's Word

Biblica provides God's Word to people through translation, publishing and Bible engagement in Africa, Asia Pacific, Europe, Latin America, Middle East, and North America. Through its worldwide reach, Biblica engages people with God's Word so that their lives are transformed through a relationship with Jesus Christ.

Biblica Publishing
We welcome your questions and comments.

1820 Jet Stream Drive, Colorado Springs, CO 80921 USA
www.Biblica.com

A Cat and Dog Look at the Cross
ISBN-13: 978-1-60657-086-9

13 12 11 / 6 5 4 3 2 1

Published in 2011 by Biblica, Inc.™

A catalog record for this book is available through the Library of Congress.

Printed in the United States of America

Contents

Preface

My eighty-six-year-old mother told a joke at the dinner table one day that has revolutionized my teaching ministry. Here it is:

A dog says, "You pet me, you feed me, you shelter me, you love me. You must be God." A cat says the exact same thing but makes a different conclusion: "You pet me, you feed me, you shelter me, you love me. I must be God."

My mouth dropped when I heard that joke. "Mom!" I exclaimed. "That's what is happening to the American church. We think we're God!"

Prior to this time, people's lives had been changed through my ministry, but they had a hard time explaining how or why. As a result of this eye-opening epiphany, I injected all of my teaching with a "cat and dog" theme. And people not only got it but could talk about it the next day at work!

The analogy in this little joke helps us understand the difference between God-centered thinking and people-centered thinking. And because this difference applies to any and every area of life, I began to apply it to everything I taught. This led to two books: first *Cat and Dog Theology* and then *Cat and Dog Prayer*. This book continues the theme, applying it to our perspective about the cross of Christ. I hope it helps your thinking—and your life—to change from being people centered to being God-centered.

—Bob Sjogren

Introduction

There's an elephant in the room—more accurately in the church—and those of us who sit in its pews are afraid to talk about it. Why? Because, quite honestly, it's embarrassing.

Consider the following statistical realities:

- About 80 percent of churches in North America have either plateaued or are declining in membership.[1]
- Somewhere between 65 percent and 80 percent of Christian high school seniors ditch God when they go off to college.[2]
- A Barna Group survey found that 12 percent of American adults had left the Christian faith of their childhood, while only 3 percent converted from no faith or another faith to the Christian faith.[3]
- By the year 2025 it is expected that 70 percent of all churchgoers will stop attending church and seek new forms of experiencing and expressing their faith.[4]

Furthermore, not only is the church, as George Barna says, a "dying body," but its members are becoming increasingly self-centered.[5]

- Christians worldwide give, on average, just 1.8 percent of their income.[6]
- Seventy percent of all abortions in America are obtained by women who identify themselves with Christianity: 43 percent as Protestants and 27 percent as Catholics.

Eighteen percent of all abortions are performed on women who identify themselves as "Born-again/Evangelical."[7]

- In 2005, *Christianity Today* reported that in a survey of twenty-eight Protestant denominations the amount spent on overseas missions for every dollar donated to a congregation was two cents. The amount spent on overseas missions for every dollar donated to a congregation in 1920 was ten cents.[8]
- Ninety percent of all Protestant congregations have no direct commitment to, or involvement with, a foreign missionary.[9]

Let's face it, we are consumed with ourselves. As the great English churchman John Stott has said, the American church is three thousand miles wide and only half an inch deep.

I, Bob, have been walking with Christ for thirty-three years. And I, Kevin, have been walking with the Lord for twenty-five years. During these years we have seen many trends that advance self-centered thinking rather than God-centered thinking enter into the American Christian subculture. We contrast these two ways of thinking as the difference in perspective between cats ("God exists to serve me") and dogs ("I exist to serve God").

As we have seen theological fads come and go, we have asked ourselves, *Is this really of the Lord? Is it really biblical? Will it stand the test of time?* And in our quest to grow and mature as believers, we have come to ask a critical question regarding theological issues, a question that has helped form the thoughts in this book. The question is simple: *Does this theology apply to any and every situation found in the Scriptures?* We have concluded that if it does not, it is not a sound theology. Something is wrong with it biblically.

Let us give you a simple example.

We have a problem with health and wealth theology. Why? Because although we find many Scriptures where it is applicable, we also find Scriptures where it does not apply.

How does wealth theology apply to Joseph when Potiphar bought him as a slave? Joseph owned nothing, not even the clothes on his back. And even when God blessed the work of his hands, those blessings went to Potiphar, not to Joseph. During those years of Joseph's life, health and wealth theology fell ridiculously short. This was also true for the many years he was locked in Pharaoh's prison.

Since the health and wealth theology does apply to the years Joseph was second-in-command to Pharaoh, does that mean it applies only to certain years of our lives and not others? If so, how do we know what years it applies to and what years it does not?

Furthermore, Jesus had to pull a coin out of a fish's mouth in order to pay a tax. That doesn't sound rich to us. Miraculous, yes, but not rich. Jesus never owned a home or even a donkey. "Wealthy" did not describe him.

In 2 Corinthians 8 Paul speaks about the Macedonian churches (e.g., those at Philippi, Thessalonica, and Berea) giving financially out of their "extreme poverty." Extreme poverty? They obviously were not rich by any means. Now maybe the Macedonian churches didn't know how to walk with God and therefore missed the wealth part of the gospel. If so, they apparently fooled Paul (not to mention God), because the Scriptures praise them for having God's grace:

> We want you to know, brothers, about *the grace of God that has been given among the churches of Macedonia*, for in a severe test of affliction, their abundance of joy and their extreme poverty have overflowed in a wealth of generosity on their part. For they gave according to their means, as I can testify, and beyond their means, of their own accord, begging us earnestly for the favor of taking part in the *relief of the saints*.
>
> 2 Corinthians 8:1–4, NASB (emphasis added)

Please note the last phrase: "the relief of the saints." What is that all about? The text is not clear, but it appears that there was something so terrible happening in Jerusalem (perhaps a famine) that the Gentile churches in Macedonia wanted to assist the believers there. Did the founding church in Jerusalem miss the health and wealth part of the gospel too? Did the church have it wrong from the very beginning?

We also don't understand how the health and wealth theology applies to Paul after he was beaten in Acts 16. We see in verse 33 that his wounds were washed. Evidently they weren't healed miraculously; we're sure that would have been mentioned in the text had such a healing taken place. Nor in his litany of suffering for Christ (2 Corinthians 11:16–28) does Paul ever mention a miraculous healing. Was he miraculously healed after all those beatings? We doubt it. Did he just heal naturally? Our guess is yes, since there is no mention of miraculous healings. If that is the case, then how does Paul's experience support health and wealth theology?

Furthermore, the fact that Paul told Timothy to "use a little wine because of your stomach and your frequent illnesses" (1 Timothy 5:23) shows that Paul's theology had room for the legitimate possibility of physical illness.

We have had many friends in the church cling to this theology, claiming that God wants their loved ones to live to the age of at least seventy. Yet I (Bob) have experienced one of our church's worship leaders die in his twenties, our congregation's head deacon die in his thirties, and a friend serving as a missionary in the Muslim world die in his forties. All three of these brothers were prayed over. All three had the elders lay hands on them and anoint them with oil. Great faith was devoted to each person's recovery. Did their own lack of faith allow their death, or is something missing in the health and wealth theology?

Although multiple passages in the Bible speak of God's desire to bless us with health and wealth, this teaching doesn't seem to represent the entire Bible. *Either something is missing or something greater is behind it.* Or maybe suffering is just a test from God, and health and wealth are on the way. But that doesn't seem right either, because Jesus never became wealthy and we have no evidence that the churches in the New Testament became wealthy. If their circumstances were just a test that they passed, wouldn't God have made that clear?

This process of examination applies to a host of other theological streams as well. In our years of following Christ, we have concluded that *if there are Scripture passages where a certain theology does not apply, then we cannot believe it is solid teaching. The theology is possibly correct, but only to a degree. There is either something missing or there is a foundational principle underneath it all that is not being seen.*

It is our prayer that the theology you find in this book will apply to any and every situation; that it is rock solid; that although it is not an easy theology to embrace, it is truth.

This book was written to wave a red flag about something that is fundamentally flawed in the church, something that is so foundational that it is threatening to crumble the very core of our religion. Once you know what it is, you can see it everywhere. It is in our advertising, our announcements, our worship music, our sermons, and our benedictions. For most churches, it is "omnipresent."

And its impact is being felt in our marriages, our parenting, our finances, our lifestyles—just about every choice we make.

The church has to address the problem . . . or we will die. So please read on!

—Bob Sjogren and Kevin Kimbrough

CHAPTER 1
Conflicting and Confusing Communication

Primary writer: Bob

I had just driven up to the building where the Perspectives class[1] was being held. The snow on the ground was absolutely beautiful, giving me added inspiration as I was about to speak on the biblical basis for God's global glory.

My cell phone rang. It was Ralph. Ralph and his wife, Brit (note: both names have been changed), are dear friends to me and my wife, Debby.

"Would you mind giving Brit a call and telling her what we talked about the other day at Bible study?" Ralph asked. "I can't seem to communicate it to her right now. I have to pray *her* way; I have to look and act like the Christian *she* wants; and I can't just be 'me' in Christ."

It was obvious to me that Ralph and Brit had another major fight. *How could she pull this stuff again?* I thought. *We've been over this with her time and time again.*

I carried my books, laptop, and projector into the building, and the people who were expecting me took them to the classroom. Kicking the snow off my shoes, I got back into the car and pulled away to park. Then I called Brit. I could tell that she had been crying. Since my time was limited, I quickly told her that Ralph wanted me to call her and explain some of the things we had talked about in Bible study the other morning. She then shared her heart.

"Well, would you tell him that I don't appreciate him not talking to me for three days straight, and for treating me like a total stranger in our own home, and for yelling at the kids every time something goes wrong with his perfect agenda?"

Ralph, how could you? I thought. My eyes had been opened. Now I saw the other side of the story.

Just as there are two sides to every story and two sides to every coin, so there are two sides to the cross. One side looks at the cross from a doglike perspective, and the other side views it from a catlike perspective. (See the preface of this book for the story of how I began viewing life through these analogies.) The cat's perspective, which is more familiar to most Christians, says, "Jesus died for my sins and for the sins of all the people of the world." The dog's perspective agrees with that statement, but makes a statement of its own: "Jesus died to reveal his Father's glory."

Both statements are correct. The question the church—and you the reader—faces, however, is this: Does each statement bear equal weight, or does one have a higher priority than the other? In other words, did Christ die primarily for us, or did he die primarily to glorify his Father? *I believe this is the greatest question facing the church today.*

When I went to speak at a church in Lodi, California, one Sunday morning, I was unexpectedly asked if I wanted to teach a Sunday school class between worship services. Always wanting to maximize my time on the road, I gladly said yes.

Upon entering the class I prayed a quick silent prayer: *Lord, what do you want me to say to these people?*

A mixture of adults and children sat in the room. I started out by asking some simple questions to get a feel for why they were attending this class. Getting a general sense of the group, I moved on.

"Let me ask you another question. What do you think the purpose of the church is?"

Now they felt more comfortable. "To tell others about God," one said. I wrote that down on the whiteboard.

"What else?" I asked.

"To worship God." That went next on the list.

"To have a relationship with God," offered a third. A fourth commented, "To glorify God." Then came, "To train the body of Christ."

A long pause followed. "Is that all?" I asked.

A man hesitantly raised his hand. "To encourage each other?"

I thought they were done. Eventually someone else added, "To be a distinction from the rest of the world." This was their final response.

I then posed a second question: "Why did Christ come to the earth?"

Immediately there was a chorus of "To die on the cross for our sins." I wrote that at the top of the list.

"What else?" I asked.

"To fulfill prophecy." A short pause ensued.

"To do the Father's will." Then there was a longer pause.

"To glorify God."

After waiting through a longer, uncomfortable silence, I asked, "Is this it?"

"For angels to have insight?" It was more of a question than a statement, but I wrote it down anyway.

"Anyone else?"

With no takers, I continued, "OK, now let's ask, 'Which answer is the highest priority?' Everyone has two votes, one for what you think is the primary purpose of the church, a second for what you think is the primary reason that Christ came to the earth."

I went through each of the options on the list. Here are the results:

What is the purpose of the church?

To tell others about God: 6
To worship God: 10
To have a relationship with God: 5
To glorify God: 14
To train the body of Christ: 0
To encourage each other: 0
To be a distinction from the rest of the world: 0

Why did Christ come to the earth?

To die on the cross for our sins: 24
To fulfill prophecy: 3
To do the Father's will: 3
To glorify God: 5
For angels to have insight: 0

After taking the vote, I asked, "What does the primary purpose of the church communicate nonverbally?"

"That life is about God," a couple of people replied.

"That's right," I agreed. "Now, what does the primary reason for Christ's coming to the earth communicate nonverbally?"

They were a bit hesitant, but someone finally admitted, "That life is about us."

"That's right," I agreed. "Welcome to the conflicting and confusing communication found in the church. God's people teach that life is all about God and that we are to live for him and glorify him. However, we also unintentionally teach that life is all about us. God did everything for us, and he lives for us. Therefore it's all about us."

Many Christians believe the greatest issue facing the church in America today is the economic woes of the nation. Some think it is abortion or gay rights. Others think it is postmodernism. None of these, however, comes close to the real issue.

Did Christ primarily die for us, or did he die first and foremost for his Father's glory? That is the greatest question facing the church today. Here's another way of asking the question: Is life about God, or is life about us? Today's church must address the conflicting and confusing communication surrounding this question.

To better understand this, think of Leonardo da Vinci's masterpiece painting, *Mona Lisa.* Did you know it was stolen in 1911, damaged with acid in 1956, and had red paint sprayed at it in 1974? You probably didn't. Why? Because it has been restored to its original greatness. What's important is that its beauty continues to be seen by the millions who view it in the museum. Focusing on what became of those who sought to destroy it gives them more attention than the painting itself—which is ludicrous! Yet when we focus on our being forgiven and not on the glory of our Father, we direct our attention to the wrong place.

While speaking at a Harvest Group conference in Fresno, California, I gave a message based on the theme of this book. I asked this same question: Was Christ's death on the cross primarily about us or the Father's glory? "This is the greatest challenge facing the church today," I said. "You name any church split, you name any fight among believers, you name any hypocrisy in the church, and I can take it back to this concept. How we answer this question will change our entire Christianity."

After I spoke, a youth pastor came up to me and confessed, "I was only halfway here when you began your message and wasn't really worried about what you were going to say. But when I heard you say that this was the greatest challenge facing the church, I thought, *Those are pretty strong words; I want to see if what he has to say is real.* So I perked up. By the end I was in full agreement with you. You are right. This *is* the greatest challenge facing the church."

Cats think Christ died primarily for us. Dogs believe Christ died primarily for his Father's glory. These are the two different ways of looking at the cross. Until we get a clear understanding of how they relate to each other and which one is primary, churches and ministries will be sending mixed messages. As a result, our divorce rate will be the same as that of nonbelievers, up to 80 percent of our young people will leave the church when they go off to college, laborers to the nations will be few, Christian leaders will abscond with funds given for the Lord's work, and we will expect God to serve us—desiring what he can give us far more than desiring him.

So what was the primary reason for Jesus' death?

Just a few days before his crucifixion, Jesus reflected apprehensively with his disciples and the crowd about what would soon take place. He said, "Now my soul is troubled, and what shall I say? 'Father, save me from this hour'? No, it was for this very reason I came to this hour" (John 12:27).

At this point Jesus stopped addressing his disciples and the crowd and spoke to his heavenly Father. Surely this is where Jesus would talk about the *primary* reason he was going to the cross. Why do we assume we will hear the principal reason at this point? Because crucifixion is one of the worst deaths any human could endure.

Jesus knew that death by crucifixion would be excruciating. While his entire body is suspended by nails in his hands, he will need to continue breathing. The only way to get air will be by bracing against the nail piercing his feet and lifting himself up. Then his chest and lungs will no longer be pulled so tightly by gravity, so he will be able to take in and savor a single breath. Then he will collapse again in pain to hang from the nails in his hands. When that air is used up, he will exhale and then again agonizingly push off the nail in his feet, inhale, and return to pain by hanging by his pierced hands. This painful process will continue until he is so thoroughly exhausted he won't have enough energy to draw another breath and will suffocate to death.

Yes, Jesus knew the amount of anguish he would face; and therefore he would focus on the *primary* reason why he was going to the cross, not on any of the secondary reasons. What did he say?

"Father, save these kind, wonderful, worthy people from hell. They don't deserve it."

Wait. Is that right? No. That is *not* what Jesus said. Then why did we write it? Because sometimes it is important to highlight what the Scriptures do not say in order to feel the full impact of what they do say.

Jesus didn't mention us when considering the pain and agony of the cross. (Humbling, isn't it?) What did he say instead?

"Father, glorify your name!" (John 12:28).

Cat Christians think to themselves, *What? Jesus didn't talk about us? That doesn't seem right! I thought he did it all for us.* But that isn't true. Jesus didn't talk about us; he talked about glorifying his Father. Dog Christians are very comfortable with this.

The true, driving passion that put Christ on the cross was to bring his Father glory. Why? What did Jesus' death have to do with his Father's glory?

I want to place before you seven reasons why Christ's death points primarily to the Father's glory rather than to us.

Reason One:
Christ's death redeemed his Father's reputation.

In the Old Testament, God was looking like a hypocrite. What do I mean by that?

In Exodus 21:14 we read, "If anyone schemes and kills someone deliberately, that person is to be taken from my altar and *put to death*" (emphasis added). This was God's law. It was clear and precise. Yet think about David and Bathsheba. David was looking at pornography on the Web, got into trouble, slept with Bathsheba, and got her pregnant. He then schemed to kill Bathsheba's husband (one of his trusted fighting men) and to marry her.

Simple question: What should have happened to David?

According to God's law, he should have been killed—clear and simple. But what happened? The prophet Nathan called David on his actions, but then he concluded, "The LORD has taken away your sin. You are not going to die" (2 Samuel 12:13). Was there punishment? Yes, but the perpetrator did not die.

Can't you hear the typical Jew crying out, "What?! If I had done that I would have been put to death, but David gets off free? The big boys get exceptions, but we peons have to pay the penalty? God, are you not just? Are you not holy? Are you not righteous? Are you not glorious?"

Add to David's sin the sin of Solomon worshiping other gods on a hill east of Jerusalem (1 Kings 11:7–8)—for which he was not penalized—along with thousands of other sins not dealt with, and God was looking like a hypocrite.

This is why Paul wrote in Romans 3:25–26: "God presented Christ as a sacrifice of atonement, through the shedding of his blood—to be received by faith. He did this to demonstrate his righteousness, because in his forbearance he had left the sins committed beforehand unpunished—he did it to demonstrate his righteousness at the present time, so as to be just and the one who justifies those who have faith in Jesus" (emphasis added).

Why did God need to demonstrate his righteousness? Because he wasn't looking very righteous or just. Quite honestly, he was looking like a hypocrite.

But what does Paul mean about God leaving the sins committed beforehand unpunished"? Wasn't the sacrificial system already in place?

Yes, but the writer of Hebrews tells us that although animal sacrifices were given for sins, none of them satisfied the holiness of God in heaven (Hebrews 10:1). The priests who offered those sacrifices were first required to make sacrifices for their own sins, then for the sins of the people (Hebrews 7:27). Since the priests themselves were imperfect, the sins were basically still with the people, and God's holiness was not vindicated (Hebrews 10:1, 11). Animal sacrifices were mere symbols or shadows that pointed to things to come (Hebrews 8:5; 9:9). Because the sacrifices were temporary, God's holiness and glory were still tarnished.

Hence, Christ came to satisfy the wrath of God and vindicate the holiness of God by giving himself as a perfect sacrifice. It was first and foremost about the holiness and glory of his Father. He was saying, "Father, I'm dying in order to show that you are not a hypocrite, that you are a just God, a righteous God, a holy God, and that you will not put up with sin. It must be dealt with. May my death glorify your name."

Jesus died so that you and I could see how holy God is. He lived—and died—fundamentally for his Father's glory.

In John 12:28 Christ was saying, "Father, restore your reputation. May my death show them that you are a holy and just God, righteous and glorious, and that sin must be paid for. Oh Father, glorify your name."

Reason Two:

Christ's death allows creation to be restored to its original state.

When Adam and Eve sinned, there were consequences. Not only were people affected, but all of creation was cursed as well. Romans 8:20–21 says: "For the creation was subjected to frustration, not by its own choice, but by the will of the one who subjected it, in hope that the creation itself will be liberated from its bondage to decay and brought into the freedom and glory of the children of God."

Somehow creation itself knows that it has been cursed—earthquakes and tsunamis are a sign of this—and longs to be put back into its original state, the way it was before Adam and Eve sinned. Does Christ's death have anything to do with restoring *creation* back to its original glory?

Look at Colossians 1:19–20 and notice what it does *not* say: "For God was pleased to have all his fullness dwell in him, and through him to reconcile to himself all people, whether people on earth or people in heaven, by making peace through his blood, shed on the cross."

Note that it doesn't say "people." It says "things." What are "things on earth"? How about the ground? How about the trees, the mountains, the winds, and the oceans? How about everything that is "groaning" to reveal the glory of God in the way it was originally designed? Yes. Christ's death was for God's glory in the "things on earth" to be restored back to their original state. This will happen when the new earth is created (Revelation 21:1).

This restoration applies not only to the inanimate things of the earth, but to nonhuman creatures who haven't sinned. This is why *every creature* in heaven and on earth and under the earth and on the sea will be giving praise to the Lamb (see Revelation 5:13). Can you imagine worshiping with a whale? It is going to happen! Why? Because Christ's death set them free from the curse as well—and they will rejoice!

Reason Three:
Christ's death satisfied the wrath of God.

Romans 3:23 says that all have sinned and fallen short of the glory of God. Usually when we read this we think, "OK, I'm not perfect, I got it." But there is more to it than that.

These verses are also telling us that we have rejected an infinite amount of glory. We were created to glorify God and we have "trashed" his infinite glory. Therefore, it is not only about our sin but also about the infinite glory we have rejected. Our rejection is infinitely wrong and therefore wrath should be—and is—expressed. There must be a penalty against the heinous crime of rejecting God's glory. That penalty is expressed in the wrath of God. It is the only right thing to do. For God to forgive us without a payment or penalty just wouldn't be right.

Either we experience God's wrath, or someone else appeases it for us. Christ became cursed for us (Galatians 3:13) so that God's wrath would be righteously and legally satisfied.

Reason Four:
Christ's death proved the infinite value of the Father's glory.

Christ chose to suffer because suffering reveals God's glory better than anything. Why? Because the more one is willing to suffer for something, the more valuable and glorious that object is shown to be. But how does this apply to Christ and the *infinite* glory of the Father?

God the Father abandoned Christ on the cross; Christ was "forsaken" (Matthew 27:46). How deep was the abandonment? Because Christ is infinite, it was an infinite abandonment—though in a limited period of time. In suffering for the glory of the Father (both hanging on the cross and being forsaken), Christ was infinitely separated from the Father, and therefore, he showed the immeasurable value of his Father's glory to himself and all of creation! As a result, we too declare the boundless value of the Father's glory through Christ's suffering!

Reason Five:
Christ's death allowed humanity to fulfill their original purpose.

Why did God create people? We were created to glorify God. This became clear when God spoke through Isaiah of "everyone who is called by my name, whom I created for my glory, whom I formed and made" (43:7). (Though this is spoken of the Hebrew people, Galatians 3:7 tell us that if we have faith, it applies to us as well.) All believers were created to put God's glory on display and make God look good.

Yet our sins have separated us from that original purpose (Isaiah 59:2). Because of our sin, we are unable to glorify God. This is why Christ died: to bring us back to that original goal. We see this in

Romans 15:8–9, "For I tell you that Christ has become a servant of the Jews on behalf of God's truth, so that the promises made to the patriarchs might be confirmed . . ."

Wait, there's another reason why Christ came. What is it? "that the Gentiles may glorify God for his mercy." Paul agrees, we are saved for a purpose: to glorify God! Christ's death allowed us to go back to that original purpose! Salvation is merely a steppingstone toward that ultimate goal of glorifying God. This is why we are being "transformed into his image with ever-increasing glory" (2 Corinthians 3:18). It's about God's glory. It's not about us!

Reason Six:
Christ's death brings us joyfully into the Father's presence.

Being in God's presence doesn't always bring great joy. When he saw God seated on his throne, Isaiah was scared to death (6:5). In Revelation, John "fell at his feet as though dead" (1:17). When Peter, James, and John saw the transfiguration and then heard God speak about his Son, they "fell facedown to the ground, terrified" (Matthew 17:6). There was no joy in any of these people because they were ashamed of their sin.

Yet Jesus' death is going to allow us to be in the presence of God's glory "with great joy"! (Jude 1:24). We will get to enjoy it, not be fearful of it! This is one of the primary purposes of Christ's death: to bring us into the glorious presence of God without shame and full of joy! We were created to joyfully and unashamedly experience God!

Reason Seven:
Christ's death allowed him to be glorified by the Father.

Did you ever wonder why, on the Emmaus walk, Christ said, "Did not the Messiah have to suffer these things and then enter his glory?" I would have thought that Christ would have said, "Did not the Christ have to suffer these things *so that you wouldn't have to go to hell?*" No. Christ clearly says that after suffering these things, he would then enter into glory. 1 Peter 1:10–11 agrees that he was focused primarily on the glory.

This is why Christ, right before going to the cross in John 17, starts out by saying, "Father, the hour has come [it's time for me to die]. Glorify your Son that your Son may glorify you." He then adds, "I have brought you glory on earth by finishing the work you gave me to do. And now, Father, glorify me in your presence with the glory I had with you before the world began."

Christ was focused on the glory. Did he mention us? Yes, but we were secondary. His zeal was for glory to be revealed. What will be the extent of the glory the Father will give to his Son?

Because Jesus showed the infinite value of God's glory, God honored him by bringing *everything* in heaven and on earth—creation itself—under him (Ephesians 1:10). This also means every knee will bow and every tongue confess (in heaven on earth and under the earth) that Jesus Christ is Lord (Philippians 2:5–11). And all of this will happen, not only now, but also for all the ages to come (Ephesians 1:19–21)! Because Christ honored the Father, the Father is glorifying his Son.

These seven reasons show us that Christ's life and death were focused primarily on the Father's glory. Let's put it bluntly: If Christ were told to reveal his Father's glory by sending all of us to hell, he would have done it without blinking. How do we know this? Look at Revelation 5:9. Note the words "for God." Coming to the earth, dying, and ransoming people from every language, tribe, and nation was "for God." His primary purpose was to obey and glorify his Father. Yes, he also saved us, but that was a steppingstone. And though his love for us is great, that very love is an expression of glory. We are not at the center.

The key word here is "primary." Did Jesus die for us? Absolutely. Did he think about us on the cross? Absolutely. But were we the primary thing he was thinking about? No. Our salvation is a steppingstone to accomplishing something far greater: the restoration and revelation of his Father's glory. This is why Paul also wrote, "For I tell you that Christ has become a servant of the Jews on behalf of God's truth, so that the promises made to the patriarchs might be confirmed and, moreover, that the Gentiles might glorify God for his mercy" (Romans 15:8–9).

Christ saved you and me for a purpose—so that we could glorify God. Salvation was simply the steppingstone to bringing us to this goal. Note how this seamlessly weaves together a clarion purpose for life:

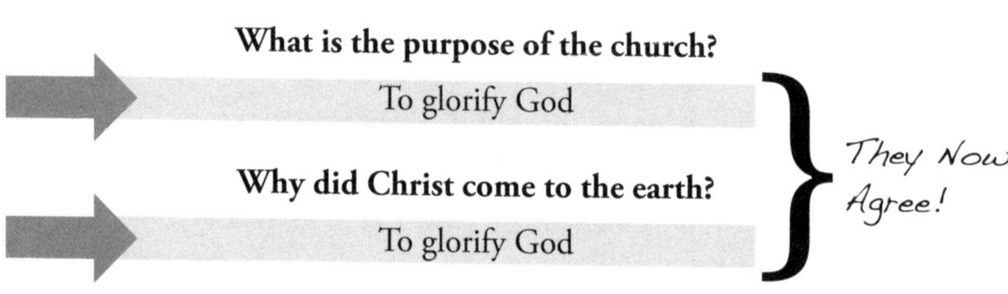

Once we understand this, we can put our priorities in correct order. We will have a full view of the cross that is not incomplete, and we will no longer receive or give conflicting and confusing messages.

Life will be about glorifying God. Our salvation will be seen as the first step in enabling us to glorify God. Our churches will rally behind glorifying God. We will use our finances primarily for glorifying God. Our marriages will be focused on glorifying God. Parenting will revolve around glorifying God. Our work will prioritize glorifying God. And most importantly, God will be at the center. It is seamless!

CHAPTER 2
A Tsunami of Aspirin

Primary writer: Bob

Nicolaus Copernicus was born in AD 1473 and lived until 1543. At that time people assumed the sun revolved around the earth. This put the earth squarely at the center of all of creation. Copernicus grew up to be many things: a mathematician, an astronomer, a physician, a classical scholar, a translator, an artist, a Catholic cleric, a jurist, a governor, a military leader, a diplomat, and an economist. (Comparing the few things I have done to the many things he did makes me feel like a wimp!)

Although Copernicus held multiple professions, his mark in history was left by his ideas in astronomy. You see, in his heart he began to question the belief that the sun revolved around the earth. He had a crazy idea: "I think the earth revolves around the sun! I don't think we're the center of creation."

Copernicus's theory was so revolutionary, however, that he was afraid to publish it. What did he fear? He feared the reaction of people in the church, because they felt Scripture clearly revealed that the earth was the center of the universe.

Oh, how cats love to be the center of everything! That's why it's so easy to focus on only one side of the cross: the fact that Jesus died to save us. Not knowing it was also for the glory of the Father, cats conclude that he died solely for us and reason that we were the primary purpose. To believe we were the primary reason, however, is simply not true.

Why is our catness so strong that we feel in the center all the time? Is it just because of our sinful nature? We obviously have a sinful nature, but the reason goes beyond that. Could it be that our sinful nature has been unintentionally fed a feast?

If you look through the hymns and contemporary worship songs that we sing, you will find that ninety-nine times out of a hundred any reference to the cross is directly linked to Jesus' death for us. Rarely does it ever say that Christ died to bring his Father glory.

Want a few examples? How about George Bennard's "The Old Rugged Cross"? Look at verses 1 and 3:

1. On a hill far away stood an old rugged cross,
The emblem of suffering and shame;
And I love that old cross where the dearest and best
For a world of lost sinners was slain.

3. In that old rugged cross, stained with blood so divine,
A wondrous beauty I see,
For 'twas on that old cross Jesus suffered and died,
To pardon and sanctify me.

Now is there anything wrong with the words to this song? No. It is scripturally solid. Jesus did die for a world of lost sinners. Nevertheless, like cat theology, it is incomplete. There is no mention of Jesus' death regarding the glory of the Father. It is the beginning of a tsunami related to our self-centeredness.

The second verse does mention glory. But it is not the Father's glory; it is Jesus' own glory. And what does it say?

Oh, that old rugged cross, so despised by the world,
Has a wondrous attraction for me;
For the dear Lamb of God left His glory above
To bear it to dark Calvary.

What is implicitly communicated? Jesus left his own glory for us! (Hint, hint, we are more important than his own glory!) "Well, it really is all about us!" a cat is led to cry.

And verse 4 picks up the theme of glory again:

To the old rugged cross I will ever be true;
Its shame and reproach gladly bear;
Then He'll call me some day to my home far away,
Where His glory forever I'll share.

But wait! Could someone sing this song focused on God's glory? Absolutely. On their own, they can cut through the conflicting and confusing communication!

Opens Doors, a ministry founded by Brother Andrew to strengthen persecuted Christians, tells the story of a Chinese pastor who was in prison for twenty-two years and gives testimony that Psalm 27 and the hymn "The Old Rugged Cross" were the two lifelines for his faith and survival. This can be sung to the glory of God. But the odds are that many will miss the primary purpose of the glory of God and that the song will be swept away in the tsunami of a people-centered cat theology.

How about Isaac Watts's classic hymn "Alas! and Did My Savior Bleed"? Here's the first verse:

Alas! and did my Savior bleed?
And did my Sovereign die?
Would He devote that sacred head,
For sinners such as I?

His second and third verses say:

Was it for crimes that I have done
He groaned upon the tree?
Amazing pity! grace unknown!
And love beyond degree!

Well might the sun in darkness hide,
And shut his glories in,
When Christ, the mighty Maker, died
For man, the creature's sin.

These verses clearly communicate Christ's death was primarily for us.

Is there anything theologically wrong with this song? No. Again, it is not incorrect; it is just incomplete. Can someone be focused on God's glory while singing it? Yes. But you have to be aware of the dog's perspective of the cross and go counter to the wording.

Keep searching through the hymns we sing. Ninety-nine percent of them that reference the cross allude to Christ's death on the cross as being solely for us and never present the idea of Jesus' words "Father, glorify your name." The tsunami gains momentum.

What about today's songs? Are they any different? Have they balanced out the idea that Christ died to reveal and reflect his Father's glory, or are they also stuck in cat theology?

In 1993 Randy and Terry Butler wrote a song called "At the Cross." It exults in the fact that Christ died for our sin and gave us new life. It speaks of the cross as the place where we discover grace and mercy, where our sins are nailed to the cross along with Jesus.

Is there anything wrong with these lyrics? No, not at all. They make a nice song. They are not incorrect, just incomplete. Unfortunately, they provide another wave for our tsunami of cat theology.

How about Chris Tomlin's song "The Cross, the Crown—No Love Greater"? It emphasizes Christ's love, love that cost more than all that we could ever pay.

Is there anything wrong with this song? Nothing at all. Again, the cat's view of the cross is not incorrect, but it is incomplete. There is no clear reference to Christ's death glorifying the Father. It is hinted at in a line about God's wrath being crucified when Jesus died in our place, but it is not explicitly expressed. Knowing many of Tomlin's other songs, we know that he is a phenomenal singer and songwriter who focuses on the glory of the Father as being what we should live for; but his reference to the cross in this song does not clearly address God's glory.

What is the big problem with this incompleteness, this catlike understanding? How does it hurt us?

The cat's perspective indirectly communicates that we are the *primary* reason (note again the emphasis on the word "primary") that Jesus died, which leads us therefore to conclude that *it is all about us*. When we start to believe that, it is like overdosing on aspirin. Since aspirin can relieve headaches and other ailments, it can be quite useful. (A cat's focus on Christ's death for us can likewise be helpful.) If you overdose on aspirin, however, it will kill you.

This book was written to challenge you to understand a dog's perspective that the primary reason Christ died was for his Father's glory, not for us. We are secondary; his Father's glory is primary.

Now we will never say, "Christ died *solely* for the Father's glory," or "Christ *never* thought about you on the cross." That is not correct either. We will say, "Christ died *primarily* for the Father's glory." Note the difference. By including the qualifying word "primarily," we are acknowledging that Christ did die for us; we were on his mind—*but we are not at the center.*

Yet when cats say, "Christ died for us," they will not use qualifiers like "solely" or "primarily." *This is because most cats don't have a clue that there was another reason Jesus died.* So by implication they communicate, "Christ died *solely* for us." And this is wrong theology.

Each time we hear the message that Christ died (solely) for us, it causes us to develop a catlike, people-centered filter in our minds and in our Christian life. This filter constantly asks, "What do I get out of this?" We might not even come close to what a dog asks: "What does God get out of this?" This filter is not incorrect; but like the songs above, it is incomplete. As we overdose on these filtered messages, we focus solely on ourselves.

Thus, when someone asks, Why did Christ die?" a cat's instant reaction is to ponder, *What did I get out of that? Hmm, let's see. Christ left the Father's glory, came to the earth, suffered, and died . . . for my sins!* And so the cat subconsciously concludes from his or her cat-oriented filter: *Yes, it's about me!*

When someone else asks, "Why don't we want to go to hell?" cats immediately start to think about themselves and respond, "So we won't suffer." They don't think, much less worry, about what God gets out of that or any other scenario.

Overdosing on the aspirin of constantly thinking about themselves causes cats to embrace a corrupt form of theology. The word *Theo* means "God," and *ology* means "the study of." This is what a dog studies: *theology*. But most cats aren't studying true *theology* at all. They are studying *meology*—with the focus on "me."

This cat-meology permeates just about every facet of our culture. You can find it on signs, billboards, and bumper stickers all across America. Why? Because in this "study of me," we cry out, "God bless America," rather than "America bless God." We say, "God bless America," because it is about us, our nation, our people, our economy—and God is supposed to serve us. There is no thought about what God gets out of our nation, no thought about how we are honoring or glorifying him. No, he is supposed to serve us, take care of us, and bless us. He sent his Son to die for us, after all, so surely he will give us everything we want.

The tsunami has hit. Cats are communicating to themselves and to others, indirectly and implicitly, that life is more about them than it is about God and his glory. We are overdosing on cat-meology in the church, and the glory of our Father is being left behind.

This tsunami of "meology" has caused cat Christians to conclude, "Jesus left his Father's presence (*for us)*, as well as his own glory (*for us*). He came to the earth and suffered (*for us*). He then died (*for us*). He went back to heaven to build mansions (*for us*). Wow! *We must be what God lives for!* And since God lives for me, and since Ephesians

5:1 tells me to be an imitator of God, I will live for me too. I'll just do it in a Christian context."

By living for themselves, cat Christians become focused on "sin management" (making sure they don't get God mad at them). Cats avoid the bad things of life (drugs, promiscuity, adultery, etc.) and set out to keep all the rules in order to receive God's blessings. Without realizing it, though, they are setting themselves up for failure.

CHAPTER 3
A Setup for Failure

Primary writer: Kevin

When our sinful nature rides the wave of a cat-meology tsunami, everything centers on us—even church.

Many years ago I had a neighbor who was good at what he did and made lots of money doing it. Although Tim (not his real name) was a great person, he was hard to get to know. Deep down inside, he was insecure. He never opened up about anything personal. Tim never shared his feelings, much less any hurts or failures. You could barely get to know him beyond his successful professional career.

One time Tim and I spent a full day together, doing physical activities, ending with dinner and some relaxation. It was in that context that I asked some pointed questions to see if he would open up about his personal life. The Holy Spirit enabled Tim to share his heart a bit with me for the very first time. I learned that many years earlier Tim's father had died at an early age. He responded to his father's death by saying to God, "If this is how you treat your people, I'm out of here." Tim turned away from God because his father had died so young.

During this conversation we talked about Tim's two children, a ten-year-old daughter and an eight-year-old son. Tim shared how he was realizing that his choice to say no to God had influenced his kids. They knew nothing of God and didn't know how to say yes or no to God on their own.

For the first time in years, Tim and his wife began looking for a church. What was their motivation? They were worried about their kids.

Tim's story is similar, no doubt, to that of millions of others across the nation. Many people go to church for the sake of their children. Others go because they want to find a Christian spouse or because they have marriage problems. Perhaps others go because they want their business to be blessed—and the church is a great source for contacts.

Many are thinking along these lines: *If I go to church, my children will learn to obey me, my daughter won't get pregnant, and my son won't do drugs. I'll also get the latest tips on how to keep my marriage healthy, and God will bless my business. And on top of all that, I'll live a long and happy life. This is terrific. I think I'm going to like following God! (And it will honor him too, of course.)*

These people get involved in the church because, subconsciously, they think it is all about them and they believe God can help them. They are entering the church with a cat mentality.

Does God want to rebuke them? Is he saying, "Hey, you're coming to me with all the wrong motives"? No. Jesus said, "Come to me, all you who are weary and burdened, and I will give you rest" (Matthew 11:28). God loves us, and he takes each and every one of us right where we are, as cats, and seeks to move us to the next level of living for him.

Although they enter the church with this kind of attitude, the "disciple-making" process God calls us to in the Scriptures is supposed to take them from a cat's self-centered perspective to a dog's understanding of dying to self and living to glorify God. Is this what happens in most churches?

Unfortunately, instead of helping disciple new believers toward maturity, most churches perpetuate the problem of cat-meology. How? Through conflicting and confusing communication, many churches communicate that life is still all about us.

I was driving by a church one day and saw the sign out front. It read, "We're making room for you." They were obviously in the middle of a building campaign. But what did they communicate implicitly? "It's all about you. We are doing this for you!"

Just go to Google images, type in "church signs," and read the results.

"Tired of being a loser? Turn to God." What does that communicate indirectly? "You don't want to be a loser, do you?"

Another sign says, "Free trip to heaven. Details inside." What does that communicate? "You don't want to go to hell, do you?"

"Jesus can turn your life around!" Again, what is that saying? "God wants to make sure your life isn't a mess. He's in this for you!"

Cat-meology is not only perpetuated through the sayings on church signs. Many church activities also quietly communicate, "It's all about you."

"Want a better marriage? We've got marriage seminars!"

"Worried about your kids? We've got parenting seminars!"

"Is your business hurting? We've got leadership and business seminars!"

"It's all about you!"

Are these kinds of church activities wrong? No. Is marketing directed toward people's selfish side wrong? No, not at all. What can be wrong is our motive for doing these things. Are we doing them primarily to help people or to bring glory to God? Do we want our kids to be good for our sake (so we will not be embarrassed) or for God's sake (so they will glorify him)? Do we want our marriages to be healthy for our sake (so we are happy) or for God's sake (to reveal his glory)? Do we want to be successful leaders and businesspeople in order to make us look good or to make God look good? Is it about us, or is it about God?

Because most churches are focused only on the cat's side of the cross, you will find very few churches hosting seminars like "Suffering for God's Glory," or "Going Overseas for God's Glory," or

"Raising Godly Children for Worldwide Ministry." They don't exist simply because most churches don't have a vision for the other side of the cross.

Since there are two ways of looking at the cross, everything can be done in the church with two totally opposite motivations, depending on whether we're focused on a dog's perspective or a cat's perspective.

What ends up happening in the church if we communicate that it's all about people? Parishioners walk in selfishness and live out their Christianity with a cat's mindset. In a nutshell, they keep believing, "It's all about us! If we obey the rules (do the dos and don't do the don'ts), bad things won't happen to us. Instead, good things will happen to us. Christ died for us, and he lives for us."

All of this sets churches and believers up for failure. Why?

Let's consider an imaginary family of four. We will call the husband John, the wife Debbie, and the kids Sarah and Justin. This family was full of selfish motives when it began attending church, and it was never challenged to grow beyond that.

In starting its Christian venture, the family had to choose a church. What criteria did they use in their decision making? McDonald's had taught them, "I'm lovin' it—sandwiches, snacks, drinks, and desserts. The choice is yours!" 7-Eleven gave them nine different coffees to choose from. They had enjoyed the progression of getting an iPod, an iPhone, and an iPad.

Meanwhile, Burger King said, "Have it your way! You have the right to have what you want, exactly when you want it. Because on the menu of life, you are 'Today's Special.' And tomorrow's. And the day after that. Yes, that's right. We may be the King, but you, my friend, are the almighty ruler." Even Dr. Phil, Oprah, and other "success speakers" told them that it was all about them.

So, of course, when they began searching for a church, they had one key question: Would they like it? Remember, it was still all about them.

John, Debbie, and their kids visited the first church, but they didn't like it because the style of music was too outdated. The second church's music was too loud. There was hope for the third, but they didn't like the youth building. It looked worn and dirty. The fourth church had excellent music and a great youth ministry, but they felt too judged by the sermon, so they crossed that one off their list.

After months of searching, they finally found a church the whole family liked. They were initially attracted to the sign out front that said, "We're making room for you!" Reading that somehow made them feel good. So they decided to give it a shot. The people seemed friendly, greeting the family with statements like, "We're so glad you've come to our church. We hope you're really blessed and that you really feel at home here." That made them feel good too.

They noticed that the sanctuary had just been redone. They read in the bulletin about the church's strong youth and children's ministry. And the sermon made all four of them feel good about themselves.

During the prayer for the offering, a pastor prayed, "Lord, we give these offerings as a token to you, knowing that you have promised to bless us back. In Jesus' name. Amen." What a concept! It even prompted them to make a small donation.

When John and Debbie heard the announcements, those too somehow gave them a good feeling. "Today at 2 p.m. the seniors are going on an outing to enjoy the botanical gardens. At 3 p.m. the youth are going to have fun at the Slaters' pool. And don't miss tonight's message, 'How God Wants to Bless Your Children.' You're going to love it!"

Finally, the pastor gave the benediction: "Now may the God of hope, who loves you infinitely, and who died to give you new life, fill you with hope and peace and joy that you might live life to its fullest. Amen." They even felt good leaving.

The bottom line is that they joined the church.

Knowing that Christians have high standards (Christians are known first and foremost in the non-Christian world for being judgmental), John and Debbie were fully aware that they would have to learn a list of dos and don'ts. Their goal was to figure out what those were so they could abide by them. Then God would take care of them and bless them and their kids. After all, that's what God is supposed to do.

Within the first year, John and Debbie got saved because they didn't want to go to hell. Their pastor really emphasized that. Over the years, they attended the church's parenting seminars so their kids would be successful in life. They attended the marriage seminars so they would be happy and fulfilled in their marriage. They attended the business seminars so their business would prosper and they could buy a second home on the lake, where they could experience quality family time.

However, between soccer, football, ballet, tae kwon do, and other activities the kids became involved in, there was little time left for God other than on Sunday morning. When Sarah and Justin grew older, they gave God some more time on Thursday nights when one of their parents dropped them off at youth group. (John and Debbie hoped the youth pastor would teach their kids the ways of God.)

Throughout the first five years, John and Debbie and their kids heard little from their church leadership about living to glorify God. They were only taught cat-meology, with the focus on having safe, happy, successful lives. John and Debbie did care for others. This was reflected in their hope that as they enjoyed successful lives their neighbors and coworkers would see their happiness and success and be attracted to the church as well.

Little did John and Debbie know that the meology they brought from their consumer-driven culture carried right over into their Christianity. With the help of the church leadership, they focused only on the cat's side of the cross. They had no idea there even was another side.

John and Debbie's Christian life consisted of going to church faithfully and even volunteering in their Sunday school class. They expected God to bless them abundantly because, in their thinking, they were following the rules. They expected that they wouldn't divorce, that their business would be blessed, that their kids wouldn't turn out bad, and that they would live long enough to see their grandchildren grow up.

John and Debbie's subconscious motto was *God, we're doing our part; now you do yours.* Little did they know that they were trying to control God and that they had set themselves up for failure.

The church had failed John and Debbie by violating a scriptural principle found in Deuteronomy 12:32: "See that you do all I command you; do not add to it or take away from it." The church had *taken away* the idea of living for the glory of God. Everything the leaders of the church taught was correct, but they omitted the foundation of God's glory. Just as any building crumbles without a foundation, the lives of John, Debbie, Sarah, and Justin slowly began to break apart until they came tumbling down. Where did the crumbling begin?

Because more is *caught* than *taught*, what John and Debbie and the church implicitly communicated to their children was "It's all about you." How did this happen?

The youth pastor prayed, "Lord, teach them that it's cool to be a Christian." Sarah and Justin wanted to be cool, so they gave their lives to the Lord. Each Sunday school lesson and youth group meeting was extremely entertaining (it's what got them and others in the door), and so they kept coming because it was "clean" entertainment. And because Jesus could help them get good grades, they began praying over every test. Without knowing it, they too, like their parents, grew up living for themselves in a Christian context.

Eventually Sarah and Justin became teenagers and needed to find out who they were on their own. Because Sarah felt it had always been about her (which is what the church and her parents had unintentionally taught her), she felt the need to try things outside of the rules to see if they would make her happier. (*After all,* she thought,

God wants me to be happy. He died for me. And I'll be happy in heaven, so God must want the same thing for me here on earth.) She did this because in her infinite wisdom as a teenager she thought more happiness would be found in breaking the rules than in keeping them. Surely the rules were ultimately designed to make her happy!

Sarah began kissing her boyfriend because she found more pleasure in that than in obeying the rules (the rules didn't make her feel happy) and fighting her natural desires to be physical with him. The law of diminishing returns set in, however, so the fun of kissing didn't last very long. She and her boyfriend needed something more. They progressively began to get more physical, and . . . well, you get the picture. Sarah got pregnant—the very thing John and Debbie had hoped would never happen.

When John and Debbie found out, they blew up. Why? Because as cats they were worried about how the situation affected *them*. Remember, life was still about *them*. They felt embarrassed and began to wonder, *How are our churchgoing friends going to view us now? What will they say behind our backs? Maybe we should switch churches. We know abortion is wrong, but if we did it quickly and quietly maybe no one would find out.*

Hostility arose between Sarah and her parents, so much so that the tension could be cut with a knife. It wasn't a pretty picture. *Is this really what God wants for us?* they quietly questioned. (Note how the question kept them at the center. They were never challenged to think about how God could get glory through any of this.)

Because the fighting went on day after day, Sarah finally gave up and moved in with her boyfriend. Sarah became the prodigal daughter since life for her was always about living for herself and never about glorifying God. What would make her the happiest? Sarah felt she would find more happiness apart from God's rules than she would within God's rules. She chose to live with her loving boyfriend rather than with her religious, but hypocritical, parents.

With all of the stress in the family, Justin quickly realized he was going to be loved only if he kept the rules. If he disobeyed them, he might receive, like his sister, the stiff-arm treatment. Justin was also a teenager, however, so he was trying to figure out who he was as well. In this exploration he realized that keeping the rules was an impossible task.

In his quest for self-discovery, Justin was sure about one thing: because his sister broke the rules, he was too embarrassed to go to church. There was just too much whispering about his sister (and family) behind his back. He had always felt judged by his church friends anyway. Justin quit going to church and began looking for new friends who would accept him for who he was. Notice that life was still about him—his church and parents had unwittingly taught him that very well. Since Justin had never really felt happy inside the church, maybe he could make something happen outside the church. He was just following his sister's example.

This led Justin to a group of people who lived on the "free side" of life. They had no rules. So he began using drugs because he desperately wanted to be accepted. He rationalized that using drugs wasn't a problem because, as the church had taught him, he needed to be loved. Besides, at least he wasn't sleeping with anyone. And above all, it made him happy.

John and Debbie ended up having a pregnant prodigal daughter and a son who did drugs and didn't go to church. The very reason they began attending church was to prevent this kind of thing from happening, yet it was exactly what did happen. What was the result?

John and Debbie felt embarrassed and eventually became bitter and angry with God. Why? Because in their minds they were thinking, *Look, God, we did our part. We kept the rules. We went to church. We even helped teach a Sunday school class. The kids were in youth group every week. And yet you let this happen? We fulfilled our part of the bargain. Why didn't you keep your end?*

Unfortunately, their church had encouraged them to find their joy in everything but God. They were taught only cat-meology and were never introduced to the glory of God. Their Christianity was not about a love relationship with their Creator; it was a business transaction with the Almighty. (God was a means to an end, not the end itself.) If they did their part, if they followed the rules, God would do his part.

Little did John and Debbie know that the church they chose to attend had unintentionally set them up for failure by teaching them to live for themselves in a Christian context. They focused only on the cat's side of the cross, and they filtered everything by asking, *How does this affect me?* They never sought God himself, only his blessings.

Because of all of the embarrassment and shame, John and Debbie left their church. Unfortunately, this was not a new story for this church. Growth had been stagnant for years. Many people came and ended up leaving amid some kind of sad or sinful circumstances. Others came and matured but then left, claiming that no "meat" was being preached. The church had a revolving door, and the leadership could never figure out why.

Somehow John, Debbie, and their kids had missed the dog's perspective that life is about glorifying God. It ultimately led to them walking away from him, feeling bitter and betrayed. Whose fault was this? There are three possibilities.

First, maybe the pastor had taught John and Debbie about living for God's glory, but they weren't willing to accept that teaching and submit to it. Therefore, it never clicked.

Or maybe John and Debbie hadn't heard the dog's side because the pastor wasn't teaching it. Perhaps the pastor didn't teach it because when he heard it in seminary he wasn't willing to accept the teaching and submit to it. This is the second possibility.

The third possibility is that the seminary hadn't taught the pastor the dog's side, so therefore he hadn't taught it to John and Debbie.

Who should be held accountable? John and Debbie? Yes. The pastor and the church? Yes. The seminary? Yes. They have all "taken away" from God's Word.

So how could things have been different?

Instead of saying, "We're making room for you!" the sign in front of the church could have said, "Meet God in our mess!" or "Worship God here with us!"

Something quite different would have been communicated if John and Debbie and their kids had been greeted with "We're so glad you've come to worship God with us. We hope you really meet with him. But if for some reason you don't, we can recommend five other churches that could help you find life in him and reveal his glory."

What if the offering prayer had been, "Lord, you owe us nothing. We owe you everything. Whether you bless us back or not, we want to give to make your name and reputation great"? Again, the focus would have been off the people.

What if the announcements had been, "Today at 2 p.m. the seniors are going on an outing to see, smell, and enjoy God's glory put on display at the botanical gardens. And at 3 p.m. the youth are going to glorify God by having fun with each other at the Slaters' pool. And don't miss tonight's message, 'How to Raise Children Who Glorify the Lord.'" Again, the focus would have been on glorifying the Lord, not on the people.

And if the songs had a central theme of God's glory, and if the sermon had been focused on God's glory, and if the benediction had been God centered, John and Debbie and their children would have walked away with a very different message: this church is serious about glorifying God.

Many churches communicate a cat's message: "We're serious about making you happy and successful." This is what the hypothetical church that John and Debbie visited communicated, and it failed them.

It's so easy for cats to unintentionally live for themselves and never consider living to glorify God. It's so easy for churches to preach a correct message but leave out God's glory.

A youth pastor who heard me teach on this subject came to me months later and said, "You are so right. Cat-meology is not incorrect, but incomplete. That's what's happening at this church. But the problem is, the incomplete part is *the key*. And that's what they're missing!"

When cat-meology's incomplete message is unknowingly embraced, one of two things usually happens to individuals. They may end up bailing out on the Christian life and the church by making sinful choices—for example, having an affair, leaving their spouse, or cheating in business. Why? Because life was all about them, and trying to practice Christianity didn't bring the fun, fulfilling, blessed life they thought it would. Since they were still living for themselves, they concluded, *If I'm not finding fulfillment in the church, I'll find it outside of the church.* They may end up leaving in anger or despair, perhaps even feeling bitter toward God while searching for their own happiness.

There is a second and more common possibility. Since a cat's brand of Christianity misses the joy of a love relationship with our heavenly Father and the peace of living passionately for him, people stay in the church but *live a dry, lifeless Christianity, blinded to the glory of God around them.* Life becomes drudgery to the rules that must be obeyed, and as a result people become slaves within the church.

CHAPTER 4

Lost in Your Father's House

Primary writer: Bob

I have a dear friend who is caught up in the rules of Christianity. I'm amazed at how extremely disciplined she is to obey these rules. Her life is a never-ending attempt to please God. She sticks Scripture passages up in her bathroom and memorizes them. She sets her phone's alarm for certain times of the day to be sure she prays certain prayers. Each morning is a ritual of repeating certain sayings about God's goodness to her and how life should turn out if she keeps God's ways.

Outwardly my friend's life looks great. Inwardly it is a wreck. She has very few close friends. Her marriage is always on the brink of separation. She thinks her children don't really love her.

Because her life is a wreck, she works even harder to obey the rules so that God will be pleased with her and come through to rescue her life. This is a perfect example of what can happen when we focus only on the cat's side of the cross, believing it's all about what God can do for us.

If it were possible to dedicate a chapter of a book to someone, this chapter would be dedicated to Timothy Keller. I've never met Tim, but his book *The Prodigal God*[1] has greatly helped me to understand the result of living an extremely selfish life in the church. He explores this truth by looking at the older brother in the parable of the prodigal son.

Keller shows how both brothers are rebelling against God. The younger one does it outside the church, breaking the rules by pursuing the ways of the world. The older one does it through pursuing and obeying the rules inside the church. Keller writes, "Careful obedience to God's law may serve as a strategy for rebelling against God."[2]

How does Keller arrive at this conclusion? By looking at the older son's reaction to what the father does. Consider Jesus' words in the parable in regard to the reaction of the older son:

> Meanwhile, the older son was in the field. When he came near the house, he heard music and dancing. So he called one of the servants and asked him what was going on. "Your brother has come," he replied, "and your father has killed the fattened calf because he has him back safe and sound."
>
> The older brother became angry and refused to go in. So his father went out and pleaded with him. But he answered his father, "Look! All these years I've been slaving for you and never disobeyed your orders. Yet you never gave me even a young goat so I could celebrate with my friends. But when this son of yours who has squandered your property with prostitutes comes home, you kill the fattened calf for him!"
>
> "My son," the father said, "you are always with me, and everything I have is yours. But we had to celebrate and be glad, because this brother of yours was dead and is alive again; he was lost and is found."
>
> Luke 15:25–32

Let's look at the core of the older brother's problems and see how it affects him. We can understand this best by reflecting on the context of this section of the parable. By this time the father has received his son back. It is one of the happiest days of his life. The son who was lost is now found, back home safe and secure. What should the older brother be doing? Celebrating with his father in his joy!

But the older son doesn't care about whether or not his father is joyful. The younger brother had been accepted back into the family, and the fattened calf had been killed for the one who broke all of the rules. Why is the older brother so concerned when everyone else is rejoicing?

The older brother was focused on his inheritance, since he was going to receive part of the father's estate after he died. In those days the oldest son received a double portion of the estate. In a family like this with two sons, the older one received two-thirds of the inheritance, and the younger one received one-third.

When the younger son left home, the inheritance had been chopped down by a third, leaving only the older son's portion. Keller states, however, that by accepting the prodigal back home the father was returning to him the right to have part of the inheritance. The older son's future estate has just been reduced by another third.[3]

On top of that, the older brother is angry because his father is further squandering his future inheritance by killing a fattened calf and having a party for the village (as was customary in those days) in honor of the younger brother's return. What a waste of his future money!

Do you see the older son's heart? It wasn't focused on his relationship with his father; it was focused on the estate that would eventually be his. He lived for the inheritance, not for the joy of being with his father.

If you live the Christian life to receive blessings from God because God is a generous and loving God, you have the wrong motivation. You are living out of a cat's perspective. Christianity isn't about receiving blessings. In fact, Christianity isn't even about avoiding hell. Christianity is about a relationship, a relationship with our heavenly Father, who delights in us and rejoices over us with singing (Zephaniah 3:17).

This is the problem with my friend. She expects God to bless her with a good marriage and a happy family. Why? Because she is keeping all the rules. It is not primarily about a love relationship with her heavenly Father.

Let's look at how the older brother's goal affected his life. In verse 29 of Luke 15, the Greek word translated "slaving" is *douleuō*. This Greek word means, literally or figuratively, to be in bondage as a slave. The older son's obedience to his father, like many Christians' obedience to the rules in church, was a dry, lifeless, daily grind. It was like slavery. He hated it. Notice that his father didn't correct him when he said, "I've . . . never disobeyed your orders." He was keeping all of the rules—and his father agreed. But there was no joy in it. This is why it was drudgery.

The gospel the older brother lived out was one of *sin management*. He was making sure he wasn't sinning. He had a long list of dos and don'ts and held to them fastidiously. "Make sure I don't sleep with prostitutes like my brother. Make sure I don't drink, dance, or listen to bad music. Make sure I do everything that pleases my father. I've got to do my chores, memorize my Scripture, read my Bible . . . so I can get my inheritance." He might as well have been a slave.

Why did he slave away for his father? Like a cat, he did it for the earthly prize. He endured the drudgery of the daily grind for the estate that would one day be his. In his father's presence there was not fullness of joy (Psalm 16:11). His father's presence meant rules that had to be obeyed in order to be good—so that he could receive his inheritance.

His life was not about a relationship with his father. His life was about obeying the rules for the reward.

Many Christians live like this. They obey all the rules of "church" in order to receive blessings from God. They are living a self-centered, cat-meology life in a Christian context. Unfortunately, because it is in a Christian context, it is very difficult to detect. These catlike Christians faithfully attend church, volunteer in the nursery, and might even work with the youth or teach a Sunday school class. They aren't doing these things out of joy in their relationship with God, however. Instead, they are doing it for a reward. They want, and expect, God to bless them.

Let's continue to observe the older son. Notice how he begins speaking to his father in verse 29: "Look! All these years I've been slaving for you and never disobeyed your orders." Can you hear the disrespect? There was no greeting of "Father" or "Papa," just words that convey contempt. In today's jargon he was saying, "Look, you so-and-so . . ." The older son was basically telling his father off.

This reaction is typical of cats who are in the church for what they can get from God, particularly when things don't go their way. They will respect and honor the Lord when life is going well, but when life gets tough, they get angry with God and feel cheated. This is what the older son is doing.

Deep inside these modern-day older-son believers is an anger currently pacified by blessings. However, when the blessings fail to come, when the expectations of blessings are not met, the anger emerges like weeds in spring. Why? Because they were always seeking God for what they could get from him, not for who he is.

Another result occurs from this older-son lifestyle. Notice how the older brother is basically telling his father how he should have acted: "Look, you, I've been slaving for you all these years and never neglected a command. You should have killed a fattened calf for me, the son who kept all the rules, rather than killing it for your son who broke all the rules. Are you crazy?! What are you thinking?"

Although most of us would never openly admit it, we Christians can be great at telling God what to do. We usually do so in the form of prayer: "Dear Lord, here's what I'd like you to do for me." There is very little worship. There is very little praise. Cats' prayers are far more like a business transaction: "Let's get down to business here and talk about what I want." Why? Because it was never about relationship. It was always about blessing.

You can observe this in the way "older brothers" in the church live for God. For them, living for God is like taking out a sheet of paper, writing down exactly how they are going to serve and obey God, signing it, and then asking God to bless their plans. They are telling God how they will follow him. In true Christianity, however, living for God means signing a blank sheet of paper and asking God to fill in the details of how you are to serve and obey him. The two are shockingly different.

Jim Sheffield, who is on staff with Global Focus, described his experience living with the older-brother mindset. When he was first introduced to this material in my office, he shared, "While I was in high school, I lived the Christian life by trying to stay out of trouble." If he didn't blow it, he thought he would receive God's blessings.

This is how many cat Christians are living: Don't blow it and God will bless you. Oh, how far short that falls.

This chapter doesn't do justice to Tim Keller's phenomenal insights. I have only hit the tip of his profound thoughts. If you haven't read *The Prodigal God*, I highly encourage you to do so. It is a must-read!

I have alluded to Keller's book because he paints a tremendously graphic picture of what happens to believers when they focus on the cat's side of the cross. It becomes all about them. As their lives progress, if the blessings don't come at the right time or as they expect, they experience anger, bitterness, and resentment toward God.

Don't become an "older brother."

CHAPTER 5
Loving God and Loving People

Primary writer: Kevin

Older brothers are far more interested in rules than relationship. As a result, they have caused a lot of damage inside—and outside—the church.

I have a dear friend who has four wonderful daughters. But the third child, unfortunately, is having trouble understanding the essence of Christianity because her sisters are "perfect" in her eyes. "Do you know how hard it is to be a Christian in this family?" she asks.

As I talked with her, she shared some of her frustrations. "I once wrote on my Facebook page to my closest friend, 'I feel like sh--.' My oldest sister found out and began to criticize me for using the word 'sh--.' She didn't even freakin' care about how I was feeling; she was just worried about the fact that I said 'sh--.'"

Sometimes we Christians can get so caught up in the rules that *we forget that life is about loving God and loving people.* When we feed on a consistent diet of living up to those rules, we can end up loving the rules more than we love Christ himself, and we can become blind to how unloving we actually are. Like the older son, we need to learn that life is not about rules; it is about relationship.

Because Bob and I are missions mobilizers, we have the privilege of experiencing many different worship settings in a wide variety of churches. During a busy traveling season we can easily be exposed to three or four different types of churches, denominations, and

Christian organizations in one trip. It's wonderful to see the diversity that God has given the body of Christ! God reveals his glory in diversity. It is truly a delightful experience.

I find it fairly easy to worship God in different settings. I enjoy contemporary as well as traditional worship. I can savor the great hymns or worship deeply with the newest style of modern music. I also enjoy returning home to my roots and worshiping a cappella, singing only the Psalms. Similarly, I am comfortable worshiping in a coat and tie, or in jeans and a polo shirt, or, like I did during a summer project in Hawaii, in shorts and a T-shirt on the beach.

I believe the freedoms and differences of each setting should be enjoyed and appreciated. Unfortunately, though, I have observed something very clearly in my travels. Many of the people worshiping in these various settings look down on those who don't worship exactly the way they do. They implicitly declare to those who attend their services, "If you don't subscribe to the same style of worship or the same definition of appropriate dress as we do, your faith may not be genuine."

Many believers are in love with their rules more than they are with Jesus.

When Kathleen and I moved our family from Arkansas to Florida, we sought a church that honored God and lived for his glory. Visiting a number of churches, we found that each one seemed to have its own set of defining doctrines. Some of the differences were minor; others were major. When I asked what the reasons were for the differences, I was almost always given a sound biblical answer for that church's particular tradition or interpretation.

I also noticed differences from one church to the next in what was perceived as acceptable behavior for Christians: how you should dress, what you should sing, how you should worship. I found it interesting that the opinions for this unwritten code of conduct were just as strong as the convictions about doctrines. Even more interestingly, I would often hear these same people comment on how bad legalism is and how it enslaves believers.

The folks in each church loved their rules and thought their rules were right. And the people in one church would say that the people in another church were completely wrong—if not entangled in sin. No wonder non-Christians shake their heads at our rules and call us hypocrites! We can't even agree among ourselves. Sadly, as outsiders shake their heads at our hypocrisy, our love for each other grows dimmer because of rules.

I observed a demonstration of this while teaching UnveilinGLORY's "Cat and Dog Theology" seminar at a large church. Being creative with the theme, the church hosted a Chili "Dog" Supper prior to the evening teaching. It was a lot of fun. I fixed a plate and grabbed a seat, and some of the church leaders joined me. As is often the case at a large table, several conversations were going on at once; and my attention moved from one conversation to another.

At one point I began listening to the pastor next to me speaking to the leader next to him. He remarked that he had observed a couple of church members smoking behind the family life center. He spoke harshly about the inappropriateness of their behavior, particularly at church. Clearly this man had certain unwritten rules about acceptable behaviors, and smoking was not acceptable.

I couldn't help but notice the plates in front of this pastor. One held three chili dogs and a pile of Fritos, while the other sported a generous slice of cake. Now these two men didn't look—how shall I say it?—in need of even one chili dog, let alone three. Their conversation made a significant impression on me. Apparently the pastor believed that smoking broke the rules but gluttony did not.

Quite often our adherence to some rules and our disregard for others blind us to our own hypocrisy.

One time I was at a mission organization's retreat when the speaker mentioned some attire that might not be appropriate for women to wear. During a break, I was standing near the speaker when a woman from the audience came up and spoke to him. She said she felt that particular point could be construed as judgmental. She explained that she had grown up in a conservative church and felt that it was a very legalistic environment, stunting her spiritual growth for years. Eventually she came to understand God's grace fully and was loosed from the bonds of legalism.

I shared my history of legalism with her and how I was growing out of it as well. While talking with her I mentioned some of the freedoms I sometimes take, such as smoking a cigar or having a beer or a glass of wine. Upon hearing that, she looked at me and said, "Well, I don't agree with *that*!"

She was free from certain rules (regarding dress), but not from others (regarding smoking a cigar or having a drink on occasion).

There are times when our rules, and especially the hypocrisy that can accompany them, hurt far more than they help. Maybe that is what the writer of Hebrews meant when he admonished us to be sure we are "fixing our eyes on Jesus" (Hebrews 12:2)—not on rules! Maybe a lot of us mistakenly make it *all about the rules* when God wants it to be *all about him*.

Are believers today the only ones who have fallen into the trap of focusing more on the rules than on God himself? Hardly. A look at Jesus' life and ministry shows that many people were so focused on the rules that they missed the God of the universe in flesh and blood in front of them. In fact, it appears that much of Jesus' ministry was focused on this issue. In the Sermon on the Mount he went to great lengths to counter those who thought they had kept the rules. In Matthew 5:22, Jesus, loosely paraphrased, said, "Do you think you have kept the rules because you haven't committed the literal act of murder? Think again. If you've gotten angry at someone, you have committed murder in your heart!"

What did Jesus do when he wasn't preaching to the rules people? It appears that he spent a fair amount of time at parties. We know that the Jewish religious leaders said he was "a glutton and a drunkard, a friend of tax collectors and sinners" (Matthew 11:19).

Jesus' first miracle occurred at a wedding in which he turned water into wine. At this point some college students might be inclined to say, "Jesus did a beer run." While I wouldn't go that far, I would note that Jesus provided the "best wine" (John 2:10) and didn't seem to do a sobriety check on any of the guests before he performed his miracle.

It looks to me that Jesus hung out at parties not for the sole purpose of "midnight evangelism," but because he felt more comfortable in settings with nonreligious, non-rules people. These are the ones he came for. That is why he told the Pharisees and the teachers of the law, "It is not those who are well who need a physician, but those who are sick" (Luke 5:31, NASB).

What does it look like when loving God and loving people are a higher priority than loving rules? How do we avoid the rules game? We need to heed the words of Jesus: "Love God and love others" (see Matthew 22:37–39). With that comes freedom.

How do we apply the principle of loving God and loving others? To me it means having the freedom to drink beer with non-Christians to help them feel comfortable enough to open their hearts and talk about significant issues. To me it means having the freedom to smoke a cigar and drink a glass of wine with others who also share that freedom. To me it means having the freedom to attend parties where drugs are being used and not condemning the non-Christians using the drugs, but rather loving them unconditionally. To me it means having the freedom to go to bars and dance, letting your light shine in a dark place. In many of these situations, you may be the only Jesus people see.

Where does the freedom end? It simply ends with behaviors that are unloving to others or unloving to God. You don't abuse your freedom and drink with an alcoholic. That would be irresponsible and unloving. Likewise, you don't smoke a cigar with someone who is trying to kick the habit. Nor do you watch an R-rated movie with someone who is opposed to watching R-rated movies. You love people and meet them where they are; and you give them the freedom *not* to smoke, *not* to drink, *not* to go to parties where drugs are being used, and *not* to go to bars and dance.

In short, we need to apply Paul's exhortation in Philippians 2:3 to humbly value others above ourselves. When we do that we will ask ourselves if the actions we take, directly or indirectly, are loving or unloving toward others.

As I wrestled with all the rules that churches have, one day it dawned on me that God has not given us arbitrary rules. There is always a reason behind them, and it is found in looking at the cross from a dog's perspective rather than a cat's perspective. God is glorified by our loving him and loving others. That is why everything can be summed up in that rule. That is the standard to which he has called us.

Focusing on the other side of the cross yields freedom—not just freedom for what you can and cannot do, but freedom for all of life!

CHAPTER 6

Freedom in Life

Primary writer: Kevin

The more you live for God and his glory, the more freedom you will have in your life. Cats don't have freedom; they're bound by rules. Dogs, conversely, do have freedom. Why? Because they live to make God's name and reputation great. Living out a dog's perspective allows you not to worry about what others think or about your circumstances. It even allows you not to worry about yourself as much. You are free because you live for God; you are only trying to please him.

My wife, Kathleen, and I have found this freedom, so we made the decision *to love people more than rules.* As a result, it wouldn't be unusual to find us with a beer in hand at a neighborhood get-together, a local tavern, or a friend's party. Interestingly, when I look back over my postcollege life and consider all the times I have shared my faith with nonbelievers, well over three-quarters of those interactions came at some venue where there was alcohol—what many would call an "outside-of-the-rules" environment.

On such an occasion we met Brian and Stephanie (not their real names). We enjoyed getting to know this couple over a few drinks. We didn't have an occasion to share our faith in that particular conversation, but we weren't really concerned because that wasn't the purpose of our interaction. We simply wanted to get to know Brian and Stephanie as people (to love them), and that is exactly what we did.

As Brian and Stephanie sensed our genuine love, our friendship grew, and we began to hang out together frequently. Kathleen and I didn't really have the opportunity to "share our faith"—that is, to explain the gospel in a point-by-point, verse-by-verse way. We were able to share our faith in a very real way, however, by sharing our lives with Brian and Stephanie and by getting to know them more deeply. We like the saying "Preach the gospel at all times; when necessary, use words." We weren't sure if Brian and Stephanie were Christians, but at this point all we were doing was enjoying them as friends.

During one particular outing we discovered that they clearly weren't Christians, as Brian was sporting a T-shirt that read, "My god can beat up your god." When I asked him about it, he told me that he was really fed up with the notion that certain religions think they are the only way. I obviously didn't agree with the message the shirt communicated, but I chose to seek to understand Brian's thoughts and feelings. I also chose not to react, attack, or wage a "culture war," since my purpose was simply to get to know Brian and Stephanie as friends and to love them—period—no other agenda.

Of course, for Christians, loving people means wanting to introduce them to the God we love. Therefore Kathleen and I began praying that God would give us the opportunity to do that. God answered our prayers. As our friendship grew, we had opportunities to share who we are and what we believe. We did this casually, as warranted in the context of our conversations.

One night Brian called us. A big issue had come up in their lives, a significant trial. Kathleen and I got together with Brian and Stephanie, and during that time we prayed with them. Just a few weeks later another potentially life-altering trial hit our friends, and once again we had the opportunity to be there for them. Brian later told me that he saw no way out of that situation. He asked God, nevertheless, to help him. And Brian decided that if the situation got resolved he would believe in God, or at least investigate whether there really is a God.

Through a miraculous turn of events the situation did get resolved, and Brian began to ask questions about God. I shared with him several books regarding evidence for the Christian faith. Being a voracious reader, Brian devoured them; and through that process he came to faith. What a joyous day it was when a group of believers gathered on the beach and I had the privilege of baptizing Brian and Stephanie! The friends I loved now knew the God I love.

Had Kathleen and I loved rules more than our friendship, we never would have gotten to know Brian and Stephanie. (Interestingly, Brian later told me that had he and Stephanie known when they first met us that we were Christians, they wouldn't have hung out with us, because of their apprehensions about "rules" and hypocrisy.) But we chose to enjoy the glory of God in life, and with that made new friends who got a glimpse of God's glory and were drawn to him.

Focusing on the dog's understanding of the cross doesn't just give you freedom from rules; it gives you freedom in the midst of whatever life throws at you—from a short-term disruption like having a flat tire to a life-threatening event like being diagnosed with cancer. Having this focus frees you from rules and binds you to love: loving God and loving people.

When you live for the cat's side of the cross, however, you will find very little freedom in the midst of the challenges life throws at you. Why? Because you have the wrong goal. You aren't living for God—you think God is living for you. You aren't concerned about "making God famous" (as Bob and I like to say)—you're concerned about God making *you* famous. You're concerned about what others think about you; you're concerned about your circumstances; you're concerned about how happy and fulfilled you are. You are living for God to bless you. You are bound to the rules because you reason, *I've got to do my part (keep the rules); then God can do his part (bless me).* With that goal, life in general can easily steal your joy and freedom.

To illustrate this, let's consider two imaginary men—Troy and Mike—who have much in common. We will begin following them right after they finished college. Though both of them are believers, there is one significant difference between them. Troy has learned to embrace the other side of the cross. He is a "dog." Mike, on the other hand, is a "cat," and doesn't even realize there is another side of the cross.

After graduating from college, Troy and Mike both quickly found jobs. In their hearts, they celebrated the goodness of the Lord to them. Troy sought to glorify the Lord in his work, while Mike asked God to bless his work so he could prosper.

Both Troy and Mike soon married their girlfriends. Troy desired to make God famous in his marriage, while Mike asked the Lord to bless his marriage so he and his wife could live happily ever after.

After three years of wedded bliss, both couples were informed that the first child God was giving them had Down syndrome. Both were devastated. Both sought the Lord.

Troy and his wife, Judy, prayed to God and asked, "Father, how can we glorify you with a Down's child?" No clear answer came, but they decided that if the Lord was asking them to glorify him by raising a child with Down syndrome, they would accept that assignment. Troy and Judy eventually found freedom in raising their bundle of love. Their goal of glorifying God never changed.

Mike and Barb were not as free. They kept asking God why he would have them raise a child with Down syndrome when both of them were healthy and there shouldn't have been problems with their pregnancy. They thought about an abortion, but they knew that wasn't right. Mike and Barb finally came to terms with having their child, but they never regained the full joy they once had because this child was blocking their goal of a safe, happy, comfortable life blessed by God. Besides, what would others think? How would they, as a family with a handicapped child, be treated?

In time both couples had two more children. Troy and Judy took this in stride, seizing the challenge of revealing God's glory through raising two healthy children along with their special joy. Mike and

Barb found joy as well, but their hearts weren't fully free as they still wondered why this child with Down syndrome was theirs.

When their youngest child was one, tragedy struck. With the economic downturn, both Troy and Mike were laid off. Living now on unemployment and having five mouths to feed, both began to drain their savings and to seek God.

During that time, Troy got on his knees and asked God, "How can I bring you glory as an unemployed believer?" Troy sensed that God told him simply to trust him, so that's what he did. His life goal was still the same: he would work at making God famous—now doing so as the best unemployed Christian the world had ever seen. Each day Troy had joy and freedom in his heart. He faithfully praised and worshiped God, resting in the Almighty while looking for work.

Mike, on the other hand, was having a hard time living out his goal in life. This period of being unemployed was significantly draining his savings and would likely delay for a long time his plan to buy a second home on the lake. His goal of a safe, happy, comfortable life was being blocked once again. Mike had no spiritual freedom while he was unemployed, since he couldn't understand what God was doing. Hadn't the Lord promised to bless him?

Happily, after six months Troy and Mike found jobs. Both couples celebrated and gave God praise. At this point both men were free: Troy because his goal never changed and Mike because his goal was back on track.

Two years later both of their fathers got sick, and their parents needed to move in with them. In addition to helping their parents financially, both Troy and Mike had to put an addition on their homes.

Troy and Judy humbled themselves before the Lord and prayed, "Father, how can we bring you glory in this?" The answer they felt was that taking care of Troy's parents would show the love and faithfulness of God to those who would see the love and kindness Troy and Judy showed to his parents. Troy still had inner peace and freedom. Though God had changed the variables in life, Troy's goal never changed. He could live to make God famous through whatever circumstances came his way.

Mike, on the other hand, was quite unhappy. Yes, he loved his parents; but he was mad that they hadn't saved enough money to take care of themselves. After building the new addition, he was never going to be able to buy a house on the lake for the quality family time he kept telling his wife about. Mike's kids were growing up so quickly, and he really wanted to be able to take them out on a boat and have some fun. Again, he was not free.

Two years later another tragedy struck. Troy and Mike were diagnosed with cancer. Both were in their late forties. Both were caught by surprise. Both went to the Lord with their questions.

Troy asked God one simple question: "How can I glorify you with this cancer?" After praying through it for some time, Troy felt great peace. When he needed to be hospitalized, he even witnessed to the nurses who took care of him, asking them how they were doing and how he could pray for them. The nurses were so impressed with his attitude that they frequently talked about him with each other. Troy was free, though in a hospital bed.

In the room next to him sat Mike. He was not free. He was bitter and angry with God. Why would the Lord allow this to happen? He was so young. Would he be healed? If not, who would take care of his wife and kids? Who would take them boating? How could God let this happen? Freedom kept eluding Mike.

After this season of testing was complete, God touched each of them. Troy and Mike were healed and were able to return to work. Both praised God and gave him the glory. Both were living out their lifelong goals. One was completely free; the other was temporarily free.

As Troy and Mike settled back into their careers at a time when the economy was in an upswing, a season of great blessing followed. They enjoyed the praise of their bosses and the admiration of their coworkers. Their incomes rose significantly. And the stock options they had been granted along the way truly paid off when their companies were acquired by much larger competitors at prices that immediately brought Troy and Mike an infusion of cash beyond their wildest expectations.

Troy and Judy gave thanks to God for the unexpected blessing, while asking him, "How can we glorify you with this?" They huddled their family together and discussed ways they could use the money God had brought them to make him famous. There was the orphanage in Mozambique they had visited on a family mission trip a few years earlier, the local homeless shelter, and, most excitingly, Judy's brother and sister-in-law were in the final stages of raising support as they prepared to lead a team of missionaries focused on church planting in a Muslim country. The gift from Troy and Judy would allow them to complete raising support and move on to launching the team.

The family celebrated as it basked in the joy of being conduits of God's blessing to orphans, to its community, and to the nations. After doing all of this, Troy and Judy had enough money left to pay off the remaining balance on their car loans and make contributions to their kids' college funds.

Mike and Barb also huddled their family together to discuss the news of God's blessing. They viewed it as the long-overdue result of Mike's hard work going clear back to his college days. Excitement overflowed when they shared that the time had finally come when they would be able to purchase a lake house—and a boat as well. Plans were made for the quality family time they had dreamed of for so long.

Mike and Barb mentioned to the kids how they would love to host an event at the lake house for their church youth group. At the mention of the youth group, one of the kids reminded them that the church was in a building campaign for a new youth center that would provide larger meeting areas along with a rock-climbing wall, coffeehouse, and video arcade. Mike and Barb agreed that they would make a contribution to the building fund with the money that was left.

Soon after Judy's brother and sister-in-law left for the mission field and Mike and Barb closed on the lake house, Troy and Mike both experienced a relapse of cancer. This time there was little hope, as the cancer had spread quietly throughout their internal organs.

Troy asked God one question: "Lord, how can I glorify you in my death?" The answer came back very clearly: *Look forward to it. Rather than a penalty, death would be a graduation to the unbelievable joy of seeing Jesus in his glory.* This brought Troy great freedom. Instead of complaining about dying, he began to look forward to it. He told his friends he couldn't wait to see Jesus in his glory. He was a witness not only to the doctors and nurses and to everyone at church but also to his children, who saw Philippians 1:21 lived out: "For to me, to live is Christ and to die is gain."

Mike was angry and bitter toward God. How could God let this cancer come back? He was too young to die. His life goals were just beginning to be lived out, yet he wasn't even going to live to see his children enjoy the lake house and the boat, much less see them graduate from college or get married. He wasn't going to get to see his grandchildren. Instead, he was going to leave the life that he treasured. Mike wasn't free, and his children knew it. They learned from their father that you can't really trust God.

Do you see the difference? Mike's treasure was his life goals. Troy's treasure was Jesus. Depending on which side of the cross you primarily live for, your goals will be different; and those goals can either give you freedom or put you in bondage.

The other side of the cross can change everything and set you free.

CHAPTER 7

Defining God's Glory

Primary writer: Bob

When people ask for a definition of God's glory, it's difficult to give an answer. I have always liked what my friend Gerald Robison says about seeking to define the glory of God: "Defining God's glory is like dissecting a frog. You can take the frog apart, analyze it with microscopes, and put it all back together. But once you've done that, the frog is dead."

For years I have wrestled with seeking to define God's glory without "killing it." In this chapter I am going to attempt to do so in two ways: first by looking at what the Hebrew and Greek languages have to say, and then by looking at Scripture passages that speak of God's glory and drawing a definition from them. Unfortunately, I will still likely "kill it" in the process! But let's give it a go anyway!

The Old Testament Hebrew word for glory is *kabod*, which is most literally translated "weight." That doesn't mean we should view the word in the sense of "How much does something or someone weigh?" but rather in the sense of a kind of social weight—something (or someone) that is so known in society that everyone knows about it and respects it.

Psalm 19:1 says, "The heavens declare the glory of God." How do the heavens declare God's "weight"? For one thing, they do so simply by their vastness. It's estimated that our Milky Way galaxy contains 200 billion stars. That's just one galaxy! There are hundreds of billions of galaxies in the universe, most of them with hundreds of billions of stars.[1] That's a lot of stars!

Not only do the heavens show God's weight by their vastness, but he has named each star. "He determines the number of the stars and calls them each by name" (Psalm 147:4). Can you imagine? That's mind boggling! God is awesome in every sense of the word, and "weighty" in our hearts as a result.

Not only does that weight express itself in the heavens, but you can also see it manifested here on earth. Look at Exodus 40:34–35: "Then the cloud covered the tent of meeting, and the glory of the LORD filled the tabernacle. And Moses was not able to enter the tent of meeting because the cloud settled on it, and the glory of the LORD filled the tabernacle" (ESV).

Moses could not physically enter the tent because the "weight of God" was so great. That is heavy; that is thick; that is amazing.

This weight is also synonymous with military might. Consider Psalm 24:8–10:

> Who is this King of glory?
> The LORD, *strong and mighty*,
> the LORD, *mighty in battle*!
> Lift up your heads, O gates!
> And lift them up, O ancient doors,
> that the King of glory may come in.
> Who is this King of glory?
> The LORD of hosts,
> he is the King of glory! (ESV, emphasis added)

This King of glory is strong and mighty in battle. Pharaoh's army was no match for him, and the greatest weapons of any nation today are still like a drop in a bucket compared to him.

The New Testament Greek word for glory is *doxa*. It is the root of many English words, one of the most familiar to us being the word "doxology." When I was a child we always sang "The Doxology" in church at the end of every service. This common hymn, penned by Thomas Ken in 1674, is a short burst of praise to God:

> Praise God, from Whom all blessings flow;
> Praise Him, all creatures here below;
> Praise Him above, ye heavenly host;
> Praise Father, Son, and Holy Ghost. Amen.

This word *doxa*, though most properly translated "glory," can be translated many other ways. You will see it translated in the New Testament as "glory" (in its various forms), "dignity," "honor," "praise," or "worship."

The noun *doxa* is derived from the verb *dokeo* ("to seem" or "to think"), and can signify an opinion or judgment and therefore the glory or honor resulting from that opinion or judgment. Thinking that "1 + 1 = 2" is not the kind of opinion or judgment the Greek word *doxa* involves. *Doxa* pertains to thinking about God.

Putting the Hebrew and Greek ideas together, we come up with thinking about God's "weight": his greatness, power, rule, and might. This kind of thinking will result in glory, praise, honor, worship, and dignity to God. Therefore, glorifying God has much to do with focusing our attention on him. Knowing this helps us attempt to define God's glory.

Here is how I define God's glory:

> *God's glory is any revelation or expression of his excellencies in his provision, presence, rule, creativity, character, and/or wisdom.*

Where do I get that definition? From the Scriptures. Let me break it down for you.

Revelation

The first part of the definition deals with *revelation*. Anything that reveals God to us is a revelation of his glory. Whenever we witness his provision, presence, rule, creativity, character, or wisdom, we stand in awe and worship him. That is glorifying God. The key here is that we see it. We must be aware of it.

This happened to the Israelites when the glory of God settled on the tabernacle. Let's look at that passage again: "Then the cloud covered the tent of meeting, and the glory of the LORD filled the tabernacle. And Moses was not able to enter the tent of meeting because the cloud settled on it, and the glory of the LORD filled the tabernacle" (Exodus 40:34–35, ESV).

The Israelites could see the cloud. It was a revelation of God's glory.

Expression

There are times when God's provision, presence, rule, creativity, character, or wisdom is there, but we don't see it or understand it. God is expressing his glory, but we may not recognize it. That's why I use the word *expression*. We are acknowledging the times when God's glory is present but we miss the revelation.

God took care of the Israelites while they wandered around in the desert for forty years (Deuteronomy 2:7; 8:3–4; 29:5), revealing aspects of his character and therefore part of his glory. Yet the Israelites themselves couldn't see God's glory while they were marching around in circles, because it was revealed in the context of judgment. Sometimes it is much easier to see God's glory in hindsight than it is to see it while in "action." It might be there, right in front of us, but we are unaware of it.

Excellencies

Dictionaries define *excellencies* as "outstanding or valuable qualities or features." It's important to include this word in the definition to prevent anyone from thinking that God can express or reveal himself in any way other than "good." Who God is and what he does are not *somewhat* good. They are not *mostly* good. They are *completely* good.

Omitting the word *excellencies* could imply that God can reveal himself in a way that is less than perfect. That is not God.

Now that we have addressed the first part of the definition of God's glory, let's look at the second part: his provision, presence, rule, creativity, character, and wisdom.

Provision

After God delivered the people of Israel from bondage in Egypt, he promised Moses that he would provide manna each morning for the people to eat. So Moses told the Israelites, "In the morning you will see the glory of the LORD" (Exodus 16:7).

Was it just the miracle of bread showing up every morning that revealed God's glory? No, it was more than that. God's glory was seen as the Lord met the Israelites' daily needs. Hence, God meeting our needs is a reflection of his glory.

Presence

What Scriptures link God's glory to his presence? There are multiple Old Testament passages that speak of God's presence in the tabernacle being his glory. Second Chronicles 7:1–2 describes God's glory filling the temple in such a great way that the priests could not enter. It is evident from the text that the Lord was there. In Ezekiel 44:4 the glory of the Lord filled the temple, and then the Lord spoke, indicating his presence was there. First Samuel 4:21 relates that when the ark of the covenant was taken from Israel, the high priest's daughter-in-law named her newborn son Ichabod, which means "no glory," and sadly said, "The Glory has departed from Israel."

These are just a taste of the many passages that equate God's glory with his presence.

Rule

What about God's rule? Look at Psalm 145:10–13:

> All your works praise you, Lord;
>   your faithful people extol you.
> They tell of the glory of your kingdom
>   and speak of your might,
> so that all people may know of your mighty acts
>   and the glorious splendor of your kingdom.
> Your kingdom is an everlasting kingdom,
>   and your dominion endures through all generations.

The words *kingdom* and *dominion* speak of God's rule and authority. This, says the psalmist, is the glory of which the people will speak. Hence, God's glory is seen in his rule or authority as a king.

Creativity

We read in Numbers 14:21 God's declaration that "the earth shall be filled with the glory of the Lord" (ESV). Isaiah 6:3, however, proclaims, "Holy, holy, holy is the Lord of hosts; the whole earth is full of his glory!" (ESV). How can the earth already be *full of God's glory*, but yet in the future the earth *shall be filled with his glory*?

The earth is full of God's glory because his glory has been put on display in three dimensions—length and width and height—all around us. Just as the "heavens declare the glory of God" (Psalm 19:1), so too does the earth.

In his doxology at the end of Romans 11, the apostle Paul proclaims: "From him and through him and for him are all things" (v. 36). This means that all things, including creation, point us to God. Think about that for a moment. The more scientists discover, the more we realize how excellently the universe was created. This leads us to giving God even more glory.

We know from Colossians 1:16–17 that all things were created through Christ and for Christ and that he holds all things (meaning all of creation) together. Though people may not recognize creation as the revelation of God's glory (i.e., it is not "revealed" to them), God has expressed it.

Thus trees are God's glory on display. A blade of grass is God's glory on display. The clouds and the sky, along with the caterpillar and the cantaloupe, all point us to God—and as a result demonstrate his glory. Everything you can see, touch, smell, taste, and hear is a revelation of God's glory.

Though God's glory is everywhere, not everyone sees it or recognizes its worth. Because they don't see it, the Lord longs for his glory to fill the earth—to one day be seen and recognized (see Habakkuk 2:14). Why? When we see God's glory and recognize it for what it is, we are filled with inexpressible joy. That is what God wants for us.

Creativity is in the definition of God's glory because he didn't simply design one leaf for all trees. He made thousands of different types of leaves. Likewise, God didn't make just one beetle; he produced over 350,000 different types of beetles.[2] When God created people, he didn't give them one set of fingerprints or one personality. Each of the nearly 7 billion people living today is unique. Why? God wanted to express his glory by revealing his creativity.

God's glory is not just displayed in what we can experience with our five senses, however. That's why I included *character* and *wisdom* in the definition.

Character

God's character cannot be physically seen, but we can experience the effects of it and witness it demonstrated in the lives of his followers. When you watch believers diligently working to bring relief to the oppressed, God's justice is reflected and he receives glory. God's omniscience and omnipotence cannot be physically seen, but we can discern their effects in our lives, which gives him glory.

This is why, when Moses asked the Lord to show him his glory, God spoke about his attributes of goodness, grace, and compassion (Exodus 33:18–19).

Wisdom

Finally, the wisdom of God also reveals his glory. That is why the Lord gently humbled Job by asking him a series of rhetorical questions to which Job could only plead ignorance (Job 38–41). God's wisdom, the knowledge of why he does what he does, reveals his glory.

In simple terms, God's glory is a mega umbrella that covers everything you could ever experience. Everything is here to reveal God's glory. God's glory is his expression—and hopefully our revelation. Because of this, I like to redefine life in terms of God's glory. Read the following definitions and see how God's glory becomes the central theme.

- Creation:
  The display of God's glory in three dimensions
- Righteousness:
  A commitment to live out God's glory, to uphold its value, and to see it spread to the ends of the earth
- Sin:
  Any action or thought that challenges the worth of God's glory
- Angels:
  Beings who perfectly obey and reflect his glory

- Satan:
  An angelic being who chose to reject God's glory and seek his own, and who therefore contrasts the glory of God
- Demons:
  Angelic beings who have chosen to reject God's glory and follow Satan's empty glory
- The church:
  People through whom God wants to display his glory
- Salvation:
  Falling in love with God's glory
- Jesus' death:
  Jesus' (and the Father's) commitment to upholding the worth of his glory
- Suffering (for God):
  A magnification of the worth of the glory of the Father
- Justification:
  God seeing his glory in our lives
- Sanctification:
  God's glory being worked out in our lives
- Grace:
  God giving his glory to us when we don't deserve it
- Worship:
  Radiating back to God his glory
- Prayer:
  Calling on God to reveal his glory
- Faith:
  Trusting in the glory of God
- Crisis:
  An opportunity to show God more glory

- Lust/Greed:
  Regarding someone or something to be more precious than God's glory
- Pride:
  Directing God's glory our way
- Hell:
  An everlasting punishment for desecrating and rejecting an infinite glory
- Impatience:
  Not resting in God's glorious timing
- Spiritual gifts:
  A special opportunity to reveal the glory of God through a unique ability God has chosen to give you
- School:
  An opportunity to grow in knowledge so you can learn how to better express God's glory
- Work:
  An opportunity to bring God glory through the gifts and talents he has given you
- Marriage:
  A commitment to reflecting the glory of God to, with, and within one special person and to foreshadow the relationship between the church and Christ
- Parenting:
  Reflecting the glory of God to the children in your care and training them in the ways of his glory

If you feel lost after all you've just read (meaning we've successfully killed the glory of God), here's a simpler definition:

> *God's glory is anything that displays God's goodness, therefore building his reputation and increasing his fame.*

The "weight" (*kabod*—the Hebrew word for glory) of God displays his goodness; it makes him look good. Thinking about God's awesomeness (*doxa*—the Greek word for glory) displays his goodness, also making him look good. Making God look good builds his reputation and increases his fame. That's why I define God's glory as anything that displays God's goodness, therefore building his reputation and increasing his fame.

Did you hear a bird chirping? You just heard the glory of God. Did you see someone give grace where wrath could have been given? You just saw God's glory. Did you hug a child and love that little one unconditionally? You just made God look good.

If you want to live in a way that glorifies God, live in a way that builds his reputation and increases his fame. If you are doing that, you are putting his goodness on display and glorifying him.

God's glory is everywhere. But though it is all around us, most of the time we don't see it. Most of the time we don't know it. It is here, nevertheless, quietly expressing God's value and worth. I challenge you to look for it, seize it, and live in such a way that others will see his glory in you. I challenge you to live a Christian life from the dog's perspective. As you do that you will be putting God's goodness on display and making him look good.

CHAPTER 8
It's All about God's Glory

Primary writer: Kevin

Where in the Bible does it say it's all about God's glory? A better question to ask is, Where in the Bible does it say it's *all* about anything?

You would think that if God made some broad statements in his Word about the purpose of life, he would use some "all-ness" words—words like *all* or *whatever*. Let's see if we can find some of those words in the Scriptures and match them with God's glory.

In Isaiah 40:3–5 we read these words:

> A voice of one calling:
> "In the wilderness prepare
>   the way for the LORD;
> make straight in the desert
>   a highway for our God.
> Every valley shall be raised up,
>   every mountain and hill made low;
> the rough ground shall become level,
>   the rugged places a plain.
> And the glory of the LORD will be revealed,
>   and all people will see it together."

"All people will see it together." "All people" is pretty comprehensive. What will they see? They will see the glory of the Lord. To better understand the significance of this verse, we need to know the context.

When Isaiah began his ministry, the Israelites were divided into two nations, the northern kingdom (Israel) and the southern kingdom (Judah), and there was great political turmoil. Assyria, focused on expanding its empire, was a threat to both nations. Israel fell to the Assyrians during Isaiah's lifetime, in 722 BC. But then the final major section of the Book of Isaiah, chapters 40–66, amazingly predicts events far into the future. These chapters not only foretell Judah's destruction at the hands of the Babylonians (which would occur in 586 BC), but also look ahead to the restoration of Judah following the nation's exile in Babylon.

You would think that if the Lord was going to call out a message, he would say something like, "Every valley shall be raised up, every mountain and hill made low . . . *and Israel and Judah will be united once again and shall become a powerful nation*." This Scripture doesn't say that, however. The Lord doesn't mention unification or the resolution of conflict with threatening enemies. Why? Because it's not about them. God keeps the main thing the main thing. He says it's about all of humankind (which minimizes the importance of either nation) seeing the glory of God. The focus is on God's glory.

That is the same place Jesus put his focus two thousand years later. Remember, Jesus didn't pray to the Father, "Save these kind, wonderful, worthy people from hell. They don't deserve it." Instead, he cried out, "Father, glorify your name!" (John 12:28).

Where else do we see some "all-ness" words?

In 1 Corinthians 10:31 we read, "So whether you eat or drink or whatever you do, do it all for the glory of God."

"Whatever you do." That is pretty comprehensive. "Do it all" is also comprehensive. Combining them keeps the main thing the main thing. Whatever you do, do it all for the glory of God.

Do you golf? Do it to the glory of God. Do you shop? Shop in such a way that glorifies God. Do you date? Date in a way that glorifies God. Do you drive? Drive to the glory of God. Are you a student? Study in a way that glorifies God. Take tests in a way that glorifies God (which obviously means no cheating!). Are you employed? Work in such a way that glorifies God. Life is not about us. It is about God.

How about another "all-ness" passage? Let's look at Psalm 19:1 again: "The heavens declare the glory of God." Let's stop and think in terms of percentages. What percentage of creation are the heavens? It is safe to say that 99.9999999999999999999999999999 percent (you get the idea!) of all creation is composed of the heavens. Compared to that, this earth—a small rock orbiting around our sun in one remote cul-de-sac of the Milky Way galaxy—looks very . . . miniscule. If all of the heavens were created to declare God's glory, why would we be any different? Did God just decide on a whim, "Gee, I think I'll create something that isn't for my glory and make it primarily about them, even though everything else is about me?" No way!

This earth, along with every living thing, is here for the same purpose: to glorify God.

I hope that helps you understand why the earth was created. The earth is here to glorify God, and that brings him pleasure. Think about it. Have you ever wondered why 71 percent of the earth's surface is covered in water?[1] If life was about us, that wasn't very smart of the Lord. Did God create a planet primarily for us and yet we can't even live on the majority of it?

Hang in there while we work through this. If life is about us, we have a lot of questions to ask about how God created this world. Not only can we not exist on 71 percent of the earth's surface, but why does the eagle have better eyesight than we do?[2] Why can a foal walk a few hours after birth, while humans take months just to begin to learn to crawl? Why can a chameleon change colors, but we cannot? Why can a peregrine falcon fly over two hundred miles an hour,[3] while we humans would laugh at the idea of measuring our running speed in terms of miles per hour? Why can dogs hear sounds we cannot hear? Why can fleas jump many times their own height,[4] while we humans measure our vertical jump in terms of inches?

If life was about us, then the way God made us and this world simply doesn't make sense. It makes perfect sense, however, if you realize that the world was made for him rather than us. God must like water, and it must bring him glory. He must enjoy the fish of the sea and all the living creatures that dwell with them. They too bring him glory. He enjoys seeing horses walk right after birth and birds dive at incredible speeds. He must love to see the chameleon change colors and to know that dogs are hearing sounds that humans can't hear. Why? It simply reflects his glory, and he is pleased with it.

Gerald Robison, who coauthored *Cat and Dog Theology* with Bob, saw this principle in life and was inspired to create two books as a result: *Because He Liked It*[5] and *Crocs Eat Rocks*.[6] Each book illustrates God's glory put on display in creation with fun facts about God's creatures. You will laugh and be amazed at God's creativity in displaying his glory.

Everything is here for God. That is why Colossians 1:16 says, "For in him [Christ, who is God] all things were created: things in heaven and on earth, visible and invisible, whether thrones or powers or rulers or authorities; all things have been created through him and for him." Did you feel the impact of those last words: *all things* and *for him*? All things were created for Christ (God). Nothing was created for you or for me, for your parents or for my parents, for generations in the past or for generations in the future. *All things* were created for God.

That is why we read these words in Revelation 4:11:

> You are worthy, our Lord and God,
> to receive glory and honor and power,
> for you created all things,
> and by your will they were created
> and have their being.

Rather than "by your will," the King James Version translates this phrase from the Greek (very accurately, in my opinion) as "for thy pleasure." Everything was created to bring God pleasure. That's why Gerald titled his book *Because He Liked It*. At the top of each page the question is asked, "Why did God do that?" The bottom of each page reads, "Because He liked it!" This book further demonstrates the concept that life is not about us.

Take note and don't forget it: This earth, along with every living thing on it, is here for the same purpose—to glorify God. That is why the angelic beings in Isaiah's vision cried out, "The whole earth is full of his glory" (Isaiah 6:3).

Some people might read this and think, *OK, I can understand about the oceans, fish, birds, animals, and plants. But what about us humans? We were different in the creation story. When God created us, we were "very good" (Genesis 1:31). He created* ***us*** *in his image (Genesis 1:27), not the animals, rocks, or plants. So aren't we different? Isn't it really about us since his image is in us?*

No, life is about God. And we humans—every person who reads this book—are here for the same purpose.

Consider Isaiah 43:6–7:

> I will say to the north, "Give them up!"
> And to the south, "Do not hold them back."
> Bring My sons from afar
> And My daughters from the ends of the earth,
> Everyone who is called by My name,
> And whom I have created for My glory,
> Whom I have formed, even whom I have made. (NASB)

The prophet Isaiah was speaking of the Israelites coming back from captivity. While speaking about bringing them home, he talked about why they were created. He states it very plainly: they were created for God's glory.

You and I were created for God's glory. Humanity exists to glorify God. That is why we are here. That is our purpose. Everything revolves around God's glory.

Are you single? Your singleness should glorify God. Are you married? Your marriage should glorify God. Are you a parent? Your children should see God's glory in how you treat them. Are you employed? You should reflect God's glory in everything you do in the work environment. Everything about you should reflect God's glory.

"But what about being created in God's image?" cries the person focused on the cat's side of the cross. "Doesn't that mean anything? Doesn't that say we are special, that we are above all that glorifying stuff, and it's really all about us?"

No, it does not. Because we are made in God's image, we are to be holy, as God is holy. What does "holy" mean? The Hebrew word *qodesh* (pronounced "ko'-desh"), typically translated as "holy" in the Old Testament, signifies being set apart. This idea of being set apart carries with it the idea of being dedicated to something. For instance, when God said that the ground where Moses was standing was holy (Exodus 3:5), he meant that the ground was dedicated to God (which, by the way, agrees with the argument of this book). Aaron and his sons were to wear "holy" or "sacred" garments (Exodus 28:1–4), garments that only they were to wear as they served the Lord as priests. Israel was a "holy" nation (Exodus 19:6), meaning it was dedicated to God.

Here's another thought. When the angelic seraphim cried out in Isaiah 6:3, "Holy, holy, holy is the Lord Almighty," they revealed that God is dedicated to himself three times! He is dedicated to revealing his glory and making his ways known.[7]

Why would God be dedicated to himself? The answer is simple. If God lived for anything else, he would be communicating that something else is more glorious than himself and will satisfy us more than what he can offer. We know this isn't true. Therefore, if God lived for something else, he would be committing idolatry. That's why he doesn't live for us. Living for us would be a way of committing idolatry.

Now please understand. In living for himself, God is not egotistical. He is not brooding in the heavens, waiting for people to worship him. He exalts himself because he knows that *when we, as his creatures, see him and exalt him, our joy is at its fullest.* Because he loves us, he wants us to have the fullest joy. It is for our sake that God lives for God.

This is why God is a jealous God. He doesn't want us seeking our joy anywhere other than in him. Otherwise we would be trying to satisfy ourselves with something that can only partially satisfy. We would always be lacking, and God doesn't want that for us. If he allowed us to focus on second best, he wouldn't be a very loving God. He isn't jealous for his sake; he is jealous for our sake—because he is a loving God!

In short, God lives for God, and it is in our best interest to follow his example.

If we think we have a different purpose than creation because we are created in the image of God, we don't understand the nature of this image. The image of God is holy. As a holy image, it is dedicated to God. It is designed to glorify him and give us fullest joy.

"But I'm still not convinced," says a cat Christian. "The sheer number of Bible verses that talk about Christ's death for us far outweighs the number of verses about Christ's death for the glory of the Father. That right there tells you it is primarily about us!"

Keep these Scripture passages in context. When Jesus spoke about his death for us, he was speaking to the crowds. When he spoke about his death for the glory of the Father, he was speaking to his Father. When he spoke to his Father, he was addressing the primary reason. When he spoke to the crowds, he was addressing the secondary reasons. His listeners couldn't have understood it being about the glory of his Father; hence, he addressed their immediate needs, not the primary overarching theme.

A dog Christian understands that we have the same role as the rest of creation: we are here to glorify God. Life is not about us.

CHAPTER 9

Jesus and Glory

Primary writer: Bob

In the last chapter we looked at some of the "all-ness" words in Scripture, and they showed us that creation—and we humans—were created for God's glory. But cat Christians still struggle with the concept that since Jesus died for us there must be something special about us above all creation. After all, when we were made, God said we were "very good," while everything else was just "good" (Genesis 1:25–31). Combine that with the fact Jesus died for us and not the animals, and it must mean something special about us. Isn't it a little bit about us?

So far we have seen only one passage, John 12:27–28, that indicates Jesus died on the cross primarily to bring glory to his Father. Is that the only biblical proof?

Great question. And yes, there are many more passages. Let's look at a few of them.

John 17 represents the longest prayer of Jesus recorded in the Bible. This chapter gives us great insight into the motivation for Jesus' life on this earth and, as a result, the motivation for his death. Note Jesus' first words to his Father: "Father, the hour has come. Glorify your Son, that your Son may glorify you" (John 17:1). You won't feel the full effect of these words until you see them in context.

What hour has come? Jesus was about to be crucified. The very next chapter of John's Gospel shows him walking to the olive grove in the Kidron Valley where Judas will meet him, soldiers in tow.

The crucifixion is imminent. Therefore, when Jesus prayed, "Father, glorify your Son, that your Son may glorify you," he was praying in the context of going to the cross. "Glorify your Son [on the cross] that the Son may glorify you [on the cross]."

Put in simpler terms, Jesus went to the cross to glorify his Father. His death vindicated the Father's glory because for thousands of years sins had been committed that were not completely forgiven (Romans 3:25–26). Christ was a perfect sacrifice, replacing all of the former sacrifices offered by imperfect priests. This is another passage to add to John 12:27–28.

Jesus had one driving passion in coming to this earth: he wanted to glorify his Father. That is what he lived for. That is what he died for. It was his life. His death for us was just a steppingstone toward that goal. Giving us eternal salvation was primarily motivated by the goal of bringing his Father glory by vindicating his holiness and allowing us to delight in the Father even more.

In John 17:2–3, Jesus elaborated on the glory he had been given (the authority to give eternal life) and how that brings glory to the Father (our knowing the Father). Then he introduced his next main thought, which was also about glory: "I have brought you glory on earth by finishing the work you gave me to do. And now, Father, glorify me in your presence with the glory I had with you before the world began" (John 17:4–5).

Jesus glorified God by obeying his will. He lived his entire life in a way that would reveal God's glory.

Jesus turned water into wine and thus revealed his glory (John 2:11). He healed the sick to reveal the works of God, which reflect God's glory (John 9:2–3). He raised Lazarus from the dead so others could see God's glory (John 11:40-44). At his transfiguration, Jesus' appearance shone brightly; and Peter, John, and James saw his glory (Luke 9:28–32). When Jesus was walking on the road to Emmaus with two of his followers after his resurrection, he talked about how the Messiah had to suffer. He didn't say that the Messiah had to suffer "to save you from hell," but rather so that he could "enter his glory" (Luke 24:26).

Recently I was teaching some home-school children about this, and I asked them, "What is the work God has given you to do?"

One precious little blonde raised her hand and answered, "Doing the dishes."

"Great!" I affirmed. "How can you do that in a way that glorifies God?"

Hesitantly, she replied, "Do them for the glory of God?"

"Yes," I agreed, "and by doing it with an attitude that says, 'Lord, I'm doing this for you and with a spirit that is pleasing to you.'"

This girl, and the others in the room, began to understand. Homework could be done for the glory of God. Chores could be done for the glory of God. All of their work, like Jesus' work, was to be done for the glory of God.

Notice that throughout all of Jesus' miracles he was never motivated to make himself look good. John 8:50–54 tells us that he did not seek his own glory. In fact, later, in John 15:8, Jesus mentioned his disciples bearing much fruit. Now you would think Jesus might say something like, "This will be great, and you will really make me look good." But he didn't. What he said was, "You'll bring glory to my Father."

There he goes again. Jesus is back to bringing his Father glory. Jesus wasn't in it for the attention he could draw to himself. He was thoroughly focused on exalting his Father. Jesus was extremely humble. Instead of pointing to himself, he always pointed to God the Father.

Not only was Jesus' life here on earth about God's glory, but his future was still all about glory. Listen to what Jesus said to his Father about sharing in the Father's glory when he returns to heaven: "And now, Father, glorify me in your presence with the glory I had with you before the world began" (John 17:5).

Jesus stayed focused on glory not only here on earth, but for all of eternity future as well. It was, is, and always will be about God's glory.

How does this agree with Jesus not seeking his own glory, such as in John 8:50–54? The glory given by humans means nothing, but the glory given by God means everything. As Christ is glorified by God and as we see it and are satisfied, we experience the greatest joy.

Notice that in the next few verses of Jesus' prayer in John 17 he spoke to his Father about our protection, mission, and unity. He asked this not only in behalf of his present disciples but also in behalf of all who would believe in him through their message. He then began to wrap up his prayer, and in doing so he introduced his ultimate desire and goal for all believers: "Father, I want those you have given me to be with me where I am, and to see my glory, the glory you have given me because you loved me before the creation of the world" (John 17:24).

Jesus wants us not only to be with him, but also to see his glory. Why? I don't know. But I know that seeing his glory must be something special, something extremely satisfying—better than boats, better than cars, better than sexual intimacy, better than anything this world has to offer. Jesus wants us to see and know his glory. It is because of these words that I can sing with all my heart MercyMe's song about heaven, "I Can Only Imagine."

Seeing his glory must be indescribable! There are no words that I or anyone else could write that would adequately describe his glory. Because it is so ineffable, Christ wants us to see it.

Observe the relationship between love and glory. The Father loved Jesus; therefore he glorified him. He knew that glorifying Jesus was very good, something you do for those you love. The glory God gives is pure, nothing like the glory we give to celebrities or the glory given to gold-plated idols. The glory God gives is good not only for the one who receives it, but also for all who see it. Jesus wants us to see his glory (remember he is a jealous God) for our sakes.

Because he is concerned about our joy, he is going to come back in his glory (Matthew 25:31). As a result, we will marvel at him (2 Thessalonians 1:10). If we are among those who are on earth when he returns, we will be looking up into the clouds, standing in awe, and we will not only see Christ, but also see him in all his glory. It will be so wonderful, so powerful, so satisfying, that we will probably be speechless, wanting simply to cry out, "Glory!"

Many passages show that everything Jesus did was focused on bringing glory to his Father. John 12:27–28, our key passage, is just the tip of the iceberg. Once you discover this truth, you can dive into it and get lost. Like Jesus, dog Christians are passionate about bringing their Father glory. I want that to be my life's goal. I hope it is yours as well.

CHAPTER 10

True North

Primary writer: Bob

Glance at any map, and you will find an arrow with the letter *N* next to it, representing the direction of north. Without it, a map reader would have no idea which way was north, south, east, or west. Most directions would become useless.

The glory of God is a spiritual "true north." It points us to the meaning of life. Once you begin to realize that, passages of Scripture jump out at you that have been there all the time but have previously gone unnoticed. An awareness of the glory of God can change the way you live your life on a daily basis.

How does God's glory affect us every day? When you see what God is doing through creation, you realize we are here not just to reveal his glory but to help others delight in it as well. We are to be bearers of God's glory so that others can see it in us, and to do that we need to be changed in such a way that we reveal God's glory in a greater way.

Look at 2 Corinthians 3:18: "And we all, with unveiled face, beholding the glory of the Lord, are being transformed into the same image from one degree of glory to another. For this comes from the Lord who is the Spirit" (ESV).

In the context of writing about being ministers of the new covenant in this section of his letter to the Corinthians, Paul compared the new covenant with the old covenant. The old covenant, the law written on tablets of stone, came with great glory. It was so radiant that the Israelites couldn't look at Moses' face (see 2 Corinthians 3:7; Exodus 34:29–35).

Nevertheless, the new covenant of grace has a far greater glory. The more we experience God's grace and reflect the life of Christ here on earth, the more we become like him through the power of the Holy Spirit. As we become like him, we are changed into his image "from glory to glory," as the King James Version translates 2 Corinthians 3:18. The goal of our lives is to reflect God's glory perfectly.

Hebrews 2:10 says we are brought *into glory*: "For it was fitting that he, for whom and by whom all things exist, in bringing many sons to glory, should make the founder of their salvation perfect through suffering" (ESV). Put in practical terms, our goal is to become so much like God that we radiate his glory to everyone around us. At work, our goal should be to show others the greatness and goodness of our God. At school, the way we treat fellow students should reflect God's glory. The way we respond to our boss or to our teachers should reflect God's glory. It's all about making God's glory look good.

In order to live with that mindset, a dog Christian understands that we sometimes have to suffer. This helps us realize that life isn't about us. Consider Romans 8:17: "Now if we are children, then we are heirs—heirs of God and co-heirs with Christ, if indeed we share in his sufferings in order that we may also share in his glory."

Suffering causes us to embrace the truth that life really isn't about us. It sheds the unwanted pounds in our lives that constantly cry out, "It's about me! God did everything for me! He died for me, and now he lives for me!" Once those pounds are lost, we can once again live for God in a fresh new way.

If you focus only on the cat's side of the cross, suffering makes no sense. Why would God want us to suffer if he has done everything for us? Romans 8:32 says, "He who did not spare his own Son, but gave him up for us all—how will he not also, along with him, graciously give us all things?" Doesn't that mean God wants us to be happy? Doesn't God want us to be blessed?

Yes, God wants us to be happy and blessed. But the problem lies in *where* we get our "happiness" and *how* we define "blessed." We can find true happiness only in God. Not in our toys, not in our marriages, not in our children or grandchildren—but in him. He is the greatest blessing we could ever have. The more we experience God, the more we are blessed. The more we are blessed, the more we radiate and reflect God's glory. That process changes us "from glory to glory." This is our "true north."

The more we desire to become like the Lord, the more we should desire his glory. When we hunger for God's glory, that very hunger becomes our "hope." Look at Romans 5:2: "Therefore, since we have been justified by faith, we have peace with God through our Lord Jesus Christ. Through him we have also obtained access by faith into this grace in which we stand, and we rejoice in hope of the glory of God" (ESV).

The more I study, meditate, and speak about God's glory, the more I can't wait to see God face to face. I fervently agree with Jesus' prayer: I want to see his glory (John 17:24). I "hope" for God's glory and get excited about it. That's why I can hardly wait to die.

Years ago, the father of my son's best friend developed melanoma, a deadly kind of cancer. When Steve, who was a respected deacon at the church we were attending, discovered he had cancer, he really began to struggle spiritually and emotionally. One morning we went out for breakfast, and I asked Steve a very simple question: "Why don't you want to die?"

Steve was taken back. "What do you mean?" he replied.

"Scripturally," I said, "you are supposed to want to die. The Bible says that to live is Christ and to die is gain. Why don't you want to die?"

He rattled off a few answers, and then I shocked him by commenting, "Steve, those are all self-centered."

We then began to meet once a week to talk about God's glory—and living and dying for it. During those weeks my wife noticed a small mole on my back and wanted me to get it checked out. I went to my doctor, and, thinking little of it, he removed the mole. Three weeks later, however, he called and said, "Bob, that was melanoma. It's a deadly cancer, and you need to go see a specialist right away."

Interesting how that happened. Here I was challenging Steve to get excited about dying, and God said, "OK, Sjogren, put your money where your mouth is. You have the same cancer as Steve. Are you excited about dying now?"

The more I thought about heaven, the more excited I became. Yes, I was worried about my wife. Yes, I was worried about my children. I knew, though, that God would take care of them. Here I was facing the possibility of seeing the living God, whom I had believed in by faith for many years. As I realized this could become a reality, I really started getting excited. In fact, I couldn't wait to go and be with the Lord. I was actually excited about dying!

What was happening? I was hoping and rejoicing in the "true north" of the Christian life: seeing the glory of God.

The specialist eventually called and said all of the cancer had been removed in the first surgery. There was no more cancer in my body. So I am still stuck here on earth while my friend Steve went to be with the living God. In one sense, he won and I lost (though my days are numbered by the Lord and I'm still "winning").

There are many days when I say to God, "Lord, take me home now. I can't wait to see your glory. Please take me home to be in your presence." I'm not sad. I'm not in a slump. I don't have a bad marriage, nor are my kids getting into trouble all the time. Just the opposite, in fact. Nevertheless, I know that when I see our Lord face to face his overwhelming glory will be more satisfying than seeing my kids marry, watching them live godly lives, or holding my grandchildren. It will be better than anything I can experience here on this earth.

My "true north" is seeing, tasting, and experiencing the glory of God. Because of that conviction, I am willing to give up everything this life has to offer in order to see God in his glory. Yes, I can hardly wait to die!

CHAPTER 11

Seeing God's Glory Everywhere

Primary writer: Bob

Yesterday I was greeted by one of our dogs when I arrived home. Jazzi was so excited as I petted her and began walking toward the house. As she walked with me, she was beaming with joy because she was next to her master. (Oh, how much I can learn from her.)

Suddenly Jazzi noticed something in a tree. It was a squirrel, and Jazzi loves to chase squirrels. In her excitement she ran to the base of the tree and started barking at the squirrel. As she barked, she tried her best to jump up the tree and go after the squirrel. It was to no avail. God didn't design dogs to climb trees, like he did squirrels.

Interestingly, Jazzi never realized that the louder she barked, the farther away from her the squirrel wanted to be. She barked louder and longer until the squirrel had hopped up so many other branches that it was long gone. Jazzi was blind to the fact that her barking doesn't attract squirrels.

We are all blind to some things in our lives, and one of the greatest areas of blindness that we have to face is our blindness to God's glory all around us. We know this from our own experience, and we can understand it from the Scriptures as well.

Can you imagine living during Jesus' ministry and watching him do miracles and listening to him teach in unprecedented ways? What would you think? Today's youth would say, "He's awesome!" They would be right. There were those in Jesus' day, however, who, because of their own pride and personal agenda, called him "a glutton and a drunkard, a friend of tax collectors and sinners" (Matthew 11:19). They had no idea what they were saying. They were obviously blind to the glory that was right in front of them.

The Bible includes numerous references about being blind to the ways of God. Deuteronomy 28:28 speaks about the Israelites having "blindness and confusion of mind." Ezekiel 12:2 says that the Israelites "have eyes to see but do not see." Isaiah describes eyes that cannot see and minds that cannot understand (44:18) and hearts that are calloused (6:10). Jesus refers to eyes that fail to see and ears that fail to hear (Mark 8:18). In Romans, Paul speaks about "a spirit of stupor" (11:8) and a spiritual "hardening" (11:25). He writes to the Corinthians about people whose "minds were made dull" and who had a veil covering their hearts (2 Corinthians 3:14–15). Spiritual blindness is referred to throughout the Scriptures.

Does this blindness still apply to us today? Absolutely. We are often blind to God and his glory. If that is the case, where are we not seeing the glory of God? The answer to that question is the substance of this chapter.

God's glory is all around us. We are going to look at God's glory in varying contexts, starting with the subtle and moving to the sublime.

Though there are many definitions of the word *subtle*, I'm using the word in the sense of that which is difficult to detect, describe, perceive, or understand. Where is the glory of God difficult to detect, describe, perceive, or understand?

Let's start with something that is happening right now, the very moment you are reading this sentence. It's not happening here on earth, but in heaven. According to Revelation 4:6–9, four living creatures are worshiping at the Lord's throne. They never stop giving glory, honor, and thanks to God, day or night. This is happening right now. It will keep happening every moment of your life, with every breath you take.

Not only are these creatures giving glory to God, but they too were created by God and for God (Colossians 1:16; Hebrews 2:10), and are held together by his power (Colossians 1:17). All of that brings the Lord glory as well. Remember, just because we can't see it doesn't mean it doesn't exist or isn't happening. This is God's Word, and it is true. The glory happening in heaven right now is just as real as the paper on which these words are printed; and a dog Christian, being conscious of that heavenly glory, gives praise to God for it.

Another place where God's glory is declared is the universe itself. Psalm 19:1 says, "The heavens declare the glory of God; the skies proclaim the work of his hands."

Can you hear the heavens and the skies singing their praises? Can you hear the sopranos and the tenors? Probably not. Nevertheless, that doesn't mean their declarations are silent. Maybe they use a different frequency than you and I can hear. Maybe they use a totally different format from anything we know. Or maybe their mere existence declares God's glory. We're not sure. Whatever the case, God's glory is being declared in the heavens. We can't hear it, but it's there.

Where can we see God's glory in a more tangible way? How about rain? "Rain?" you ask. "How does that glorify God?"

Rain is a testimony to the faithfulness and goodness of God, which are a part of his glory. During Paul's first missionary journey, he and Barnabas ministered in the Gentile city of Lystra. When the Lord used Paul and Barnabas to heal a man who had been crippled from birth, the entire city suddenly assumed they were gods. Paul and Barnabas refused to be worshiped, of course, saying, "We too are only human, like you" (Acts 14:15).

Then Paul explained how God had not left himself without a witness to them. How are they not without witness? Paul says:

> We bring you good news, that you should turn from these vain things to a living God, who made the heaven and the earth and the sea and all that is in them. In past

> generations he allowed all the nations to walk in their own ways. Yet he did not leave himself without witness, for he did good by giving you rains from heaven and fruitful seasons, satisfying your hearts with food and gladness.
>
> Acts 14:16–17, ESV

Not only does this passage say that rain from heaven is a witness to God (and therefore to his glory), but it also says that good crops, pleasure in eating, and joy in our hearts are all a testimony to God's goodness and therefore his glory.

Have you eaten a good meal lately? Have you tasted a dish that was so fantastic you could hardly believe it? You may not have realized you were experiencing God's glory, but you were.

Not only did God give you the taste buds with which to experience his glory, but this Scripture says that he also brought rain to cause the plants to grow. That feeling of satisfaction you received when you harvested your garden was also from God. It was there to point to his glory.

Have you ever had "gladness" in your heart? Have you recently delighted in your child's happiness at a birthday party, or watched a sunrise or sunset? Did you feel that calm joy steal over you as you admired the kaleidoscope of fiery hues painted across the sky? You experienced God's glory. That is the purpose of those moments.

Remember Romans 11:36: "From him and through him and for him are all things."

So we have gone from four living creatures that worship around God's throne to several far more tangible experiences: rain, good food, satisfaction, and joy.

How else has God tangibly revealed his glory to us?

James 1:17 says that all good and perfect gifts are from God. Has God ever given you a gift? Has someone ever unexpectedly blessed you? Did you recently get a new job or a raise? Did your parents or grandparents buy you something you had been wanting for a long time? Did one of your friends come over just to spend some time visiting with you?

If something is a good and perfect gift, it is from God. Dog Christians realize that these gifts, like all things God creates, are designed to point us to him.

Let's look at another even more tangible way that God's glory is shining around us every day and we're not even aware of it. How about our five senses?

Did you ever wonder why God gave us our five senses? Think about it for a moment. When God created humankind, was he working from a rulebook that said, "If thou shalt make a creation, it must have a sense of taste, it must be able to see, it will need a sense of smell, it must be able to feel, and it must be able to hear"?

No. That rulebook never existed. God started from scratch. He could have made everything taste like chicken, but he said, "No, I want my people to taste my glory. I want them to taste a watermelon. I want them to taste a mango. I want them to taste an onion and broccoli." Why? Because it reveals his glory.

He doesn't just want us to taste; he also wants us to hear the birds chirping in the trees. They too are declaring his glory, and he wants us to relish it. He wants us to hear the trees stirred by a gentle breeze. He wants us to hear a toddler's laughter, because he created that laughter and delights in it and wants us to delight in it as well. He gave us ears to hear for his glory.

Our sight is the same. God wants us to see his glory. For example, God loves to paint sunsets. In fact, he loves it so much he is doing it twenty-four hours a day, seven days a week. He is constantly changing it and manipulating the clouds in order to make it spectacular. No people can even see the majority of the sunsets since they occur on the oceans. That doesn't stop God from making them, however. He makes them just because he enjoys them—even if by himself. And because he loves to share his joy, he shares some of them with us.

Remarkably, God is constantly painting a sunrise as well. He is having a blast, and he wants us to see some of what he has created here on this planet. He wants us to experience his sunsets and sunrises. Why? They point to him. They were created for his glory. He wants us to experience his glory and receive great joy.

The ability to smell directs us to God's glory as well. It is expressed through the fragrance of a rose or honeysuckle as you walk along a road. His glory is demonstrated by the ability to smell the perfume or cologne on the one you love. Whatever it is, it exists to draw you closer to God. You are smelling his glory.

Touch does the same thing, whether it is the soft, gentle skin of a baby or the rough bark of a tree. God created the skin and the bark. It was created by him and for him and is designed to point us to his glory.

All fives senses were designed to point us to God.

Let's look at another way in which we have been oblivious of God's glory. In Exodus 15 we find the Israelites just after they had left Egypt and were traveling to the Promised Land. They were exuberantly singing praises to God . . . until they ran out of food and water. Then they complained to him. Note how God answered them:

> Then the Lord said to Moses, "I will rain down bread from heaven for you. The people are to go out each day and gather enough for that day. In this way I will test them and see whether they will follow my instructions. On the sixth day they are to prepare what they bring in, and that is to be twice as much as they gather on the other days."
>
> So Moses and Aaron said to all the Israelites, "In the evening you will know that it was the Lord who brought you out of Egypt, and *in the morning you will see the glory of the Lord*, because he has heard your grumbling against him."
>
> Exodus 16:4–7 (emphasis added)

How would the Israelites see the glory of the Lord? Through the manna, the "bread from heaven," that they would receive each and every day.

God's glory would be seen in two ways. First, by God's provision for the people. Do you realize the implications of this? Each time God provides for you, you are seeing his glory. It might be through your paycheck from work or through an unexpected gift from a friend. Perhaps someone came by with a bag of groceries. Regardless of the method—somehow, someway, you were provided for. "No, provision came through my employer," cries the cat, "not from God." "Yes, provision came from God," says the dog. "He was just working through my employer."

God doesn't just provide for our physical needs. Maybe he provided a word of encouragement for you from someone at just the right time. Or perhaps he provided encouragement through a nod of approval from a significant person in your life. Each time God provides exactly what you need, that is a revelation of his glory.

Second, God's glory was revealed to the Israelites in the miraculous way the manna was provided. Have you seen any miracles recently? Was your friend's cancer healed in a way that the doctors can't explain? Did the amount of money you needed suddenly arrive in the mail? Those things happened to point you to God. In fact, miracles are one of the easiest ways to experience the glory of God. When God acts in a way that no one can explain, we see his glory. There is no other explanation. The events direct us to God, just as they were intended.

Unfortunately, while miracles are easy to get excited about and rejoice over, the other forms of provision aren't usually attributed to God, especially by cat Christians. Yet all of them are equally from God. All of them point to God and his glory—for "in the morning you will see the glory of the LORD."

Second Corinthians 3:16–18 is another Scripture that points us to God's glory:

> But when one turns to the Lord, the veil is removed. Now the Lord is the Spirit, and where the Spirit of the Lord is, there is freedom. And we all, with unveiled face, beholding the glory of the Lord, are being transformed into the same image from one degree of glory to another. For this comes from the Lord who is the Spirit.

Note the words "from one degree of glory to another." What is Paul talking about here? He is talking about the process of becoming more like the Lord. A word we often use in this regard is "sanctification." As we become more like Christ, as we are sanctified, we reflect his glory to those around us. They see him in us.

After I graduated from college, I went to Libya with a group of other young men. Harry Gray was one of those other young men. Harry was a rough, street-fighter type of person before he came to know Christ. When he dedicated his life to the Lord, his life changed instantly and dramatically. No longer did he fight. No longer did he swear. Harry was radically changed, and that change brought God great glory because it couldn't be explained by anything or anyone but God.

The good news is that all those who know the Lord are being sanctified if they are yielding to him. The bad news is that this sanctification cannot be seen as easily in most of our lives as it could be seen in Harry's life. Oftentimes it seems like as soon as we conquer one area of sin in our lives, another area of sin pops up, and we have something else to work on. Most of our growth in sanctification occurs slowly, over long periods of time. In our eyes it looks like we constantly have to grow in some area, whereas in others' eyes we are becoming more and more like Christ, and that brings glory to God.

Think of it this way. If your aunt and uncle haven't seen you for five years, they would say, "Wow, you have really changed!" You wouldn't have seen the change because you're already working on the next sin God has shown you. But others can see a dramatic change if they see you only every few years. They are glorifying God for the changes in your life!

Changing slowly over time reveals God's glory, yet it is very subtle. God's provision through a paycheck shows the same glory, and it too can be subtle—unlike a miracle. But all these things reflect God's glory. Some revelations are subtle. Some are obvious. If we were to try to graph these revelations, they would look something like this:

Little Blindness to God's Glory

Miraculous Signs
Suffering
Sanctification
Providing for Us
Our Five Senses
Good Gifts
Rain, Food, Joy
Creation
Angels Praising God

High Degree of Blindness to God's Glory

Note that where the triangle is wider people tend to have greater blindness. We might even have some blindness to miracles. Some people won't believe even though they experience miracles. They remain blind to God's glory.

Just like Jazzi was blind to the fact that her barking scared the squirrel away, so too we are often blind to most of God's glory all around us (except, of course, the miraculous types). Mark it down clearly in your heart, though: God's glory is everywhere. Everything is from him, through him, and for him.

CHAPTER 12
The Goal of God's Glory

Primary writer: Kevin

What is God's goal for his glory? Is God's glory just supposed to be seen? Is it just supposed to be admired? Are we simply expected to stare at it and exclaim, "Wow!"

No, there is much more to it than that. We're not talking about a self-centered, egotistical God brooding in the heavens, waiting to be praised. God's goal for his glory is to bring us closer to him so that we enjoy his presence, fall deeply in love with him, delight in him, and are satisfied with him.

God wants us to see his glory for our sake. The more we experience it, the more we are satisfied. The more we are satisfied, the greater his glory shines in our hearts. As John Piper says, "God is most glorified in us when we are most satisfied in him."[1] It is a win-win scenario.

This is why God is a "jealous God" (Deuteronomy 4:24). God is jealous for his glory—for our sake. He wants nothing more than to shine and radiate his glory in our lives, because he knows that when he does that, we will be the most satisfied we can be. God's glory will fulfill us more than anything else this world has to offer. Hence he jealously guards and protects it for our sake.

In his book *Shattered Dreams*, Larry Crabb basically presents the same theme, submitting the idea that God is in the business of shattering dreams.[2] Now if you focus only on the cat's perspective of the cross, you will drop your mouth in disbelief and protest, "God would never shatter my dreams. God loves me. He wants to *fulfill* my dreams, not shatter them."

However, if you focus primarily on the other side of the cross—the dog's side—you will say, "Oh, I get it. God shatters any dream we have that's not of him." This means that if you prayerfully go to God and ask him for a successful business or a great ministry, and that business or ministry becomes more important to you than God himself, he will shatter that dream before it becomes an idol. That dream won't satisfy you as much as God; therefore, God becomes jealous for his glory—for your sake.

In Jeremiah 32:40, God says this about his people: "I will make an everlasting covenant with them: I will never stop doing good to them." God will never stop doing good to you, even if it means shattering your dreams. Why? Because as he shatters your dreams, he is bringing your focus back to him; and he will satisfy you more than a successful business, a great ministry, or any other idol you can dream up. As the old adage goes, "You'll never know Jesus is all you need until Jesus is all you've got." God doesn't mind taking us down further and further until the only direction we can look is up.

Romans 12:1 speaks of us being a "living sacrifice." Early in my Christian life I was taught three characteristics about living sacrifices. First, their past means nothing. Second, they have no plans for the future. And third, they are looking solely in one direction: up.

God's glory is designed to bring you first and foremost to him. It is what Christ died for. It is the gospel message.

Consider 1 Peter 3:18: "For Christ also suffered once for sins, the righteous for the unrighteous, *that he might bring us to God*, being put to death in the flesh but made alive in the spirit" (ESV, emphasis added). Jesus died for the purpose of bringing us to God.

God is the good news! He is the ultimate goal of everything in the Christian life. John Piper wrote an excellent book on this subject, entitled *God Is the Gospel*,[3] which I highly encourage you to read.

I want you to see another example of God's glory pointing to God. Hebrews 1:3 tells us that Jesus is the "radiance of God's glory." Since Jesus died "that he might bring us to God," as we see in 1 Peter 3:18, those two thoughts combine to say, "The radiance of God's glory brings us to God." The goal of seeing, cherishing, and delighting in God's glory is to bring us to God.

Look at Isaiah 40:9:

> Get you up to a high mountain,
>   O Zion, *herald of good news*;
> lift up your voice with strength,
>   O Jerusalem, *herald of good news*;
>   lift it up, fear not;
> say to the cities of Judah,
>   "*Behold your God!*" (ESV, emphasis added)

Zion, or Jerusalem, was to be a bearer of good news. Israel was to be a Great Commission nation, although few saw it that way. What was the good news they were to herald? "Behold your God!" The goal was to see God. Why? If people saw him, they would cherish him, enjoy him, radiate him, and be satisfied by him. All of this glorifies God.

Just as the Israelites were supposed to point people to God, so too are we. Why? He alone fully delights us. He alone completely satisfies us. He alone causes our souls to overflow with joy. Since everything is from him, through him, and to him, it is only right that God's glory should be our primary focus. God is the good news.

The Scriptures weave together God, the good news, and God's glory in a beautiful way. First Timothy contains a great passage in which to see this. In 1 Timothy 1:8–10 Paul presents a list of reasons why the law was given. Then he turns to the gospel. And in doing so Paul brings us back to God's glory, as he refers to "the gospel of the glory of the blessed God with which I have been entrusted"

(1 Timothy 1:11, ESV). Take out the adjective preceding God ("the blessed"), and we read "the gospel of the glory of God."

The good news we share, which is the gospel, is the glory of God. Remember, everything is from him, through him, and to him. Everything is designed to point us to God, including the good news of his glory.

But if God's glory really is the good news, how can you share it? You can't take some of God's glory out of your bank account to give away. You can't have someone over for "God's glory," like you can for dinner. Exactly how do you share the glory of God in practical ways?

You can do so by talking about everything that is good and right about God. You can point to a sunset and say, "Look at God's glory." You can give grace to those who don't deserve it and say, "This is God's glory." You can give up your life and die to yourself through feeding the homeless, volunteering at a nursing home, or helping the poor, and through your words and actions declare, "Here is the glory of God."

When people see your life being poured out as an offering for others, they will see God's glory being lived out through you. They will take notice of your God and say, "Whatever you've got, I want."

When Jesus prayed to the Father in John 17, he said, "Now this is eternal life: that they know you, the only true God, and Jesus Christ, whom you have sent" (John 17:3). Knowing God and having a personal relationship with him is what eternal life is all about! It's all about God!

Jesus also said, "Blessed are the pure in heart, for they will see God" (Matthew 5:8). When you keep yourself pure, you receive God—not riches, not awards, not kudos, but God. Knowing God is what Christianity is all about. Hence the apostle John writes, "Anyone who runs ahead and does not continue in the teaching of Christ does not have God; whoever continues in the teaching has both the Father and the Son" (2 John 1:9).

A person with a dog's perspective of the cross knows that having God is the essence of the good news. It is the soul of Christianity.

God is the gospel. His glory directs us to him. This is why he is a jealous God. As people see his glory being lived through you, that glory will draw them to God, the great reward. He is more valuable than his blessings. This is the pinnacle of the other side of the cross.

CHAPTER 13

What about Saving the Lost?

Primary writer: Bob

When I was on staff with Frontiers many years ago, I regularly spoke to the organization's candidate school. I often began my talk by reading the first chapter of Genesis. If you ever happen to read Genesis 1 to future missionaries, you will probably get the same reaction I received. At first they listened eagerly, but then changed to polite listening. As the chapter went on, they began to wonder what I was doing. When they realized I was going to read the entire chapter, they started looking at their watches, glancing out the windows, etc.

Why were they bored? Not because they were extremely familiar with Genesis 1, although they would say that was the reason. No, the real reason most missionaries (and other believers) are bored with Genesis 1 is simply because no people are included. And if people aren't involved, it must not be very interesting.

Most evangelicals don't get excited about the Bible until Genesis 3. "Ah, there's a problem, and it's sin! This must be the theme of God's Word. We must rescue lost souls from hell!" Saving the lost becomes the substance of their Christian life. Genesis 1 and 2? Those chapters are boring.

Little did those new candidates know they were nonverbally communicating to God and to themselves that the Bible is all about them. It goes straight to a cat's understanding of the cross.

"But wait a second!" cries a cat Christian. "Isn't there biblical evidence to prove that if it's not all about us, it's at least half about us? Many Scriptures clearly say that the main reason Christ came was to save us."

Let's list some Scriptures relevant to this issue:

- "The Son of Man came to seek and to save the lost."—Luke 19:10
- "The Pharisees and their scribes grumbled at his disciples, saying, 'Why do you eat and drink with tax collectors and sinners?' And Jesus answered them, 'Those who are well have no need of a physician, but those who are sick. I have not come to call the righteous but sinners to repentance.'"—Luke 5:30–32, ESV
- "She will give birth to a son, and you are to give him the name Jesus, because he will save his people from their sins."—Matthew 1:21
- "For while we were still weak, at the right time Christ died for the ungodly."—Romans 5:6, ESV
- "Here is a trustworthy saying that deserves full acceptance: Christ Jesus came into the world to save sinners—of whom I am the worst."—1 Timothy 1:15
- And, of course, how could we forget John 3:16? "For God so loved the world that he gave his one and only Son, that whoever believes in him shall not perish but have eternal life."

"There!" exclaims our hypothetical believer. "These Scriptures are very clear: Christ came to die for us. That was his *primary* purpose."

We have never disagreed with the idea that Christ came to die for us. That is absolutely clear in the Scriptures. We have also never disagreed that he must have thought about us on the cross. What we are challenging is the notion that we are *primary*. Jesus did die for us, but the other side of the cross shows us there was a higher motivation.

How can we say that in light of all these Scriptures declaring that Christ died to save sinners? It's easy. Look at other Scriptures that point to the result of people's salvation, and you will get back to the glory of God being the foundational motivation for everything.

Take, for example, Philippians 2:1–11. This passage is all about Christ's life on this earth and death on the cross. When I was young in my Christian faith, I heard this passage quoted many times. What I heard wasn't incorrect, but it was incomplete. People always quoted the first part of verse 11 but never seemed to quote the second part. Here is Philippians 2:1–11a (ESV):

> So if there is any encouragement in Christ, any comfort from love, any participation in the Spirit, any affection and sympathy, complete my joy by being of the same mind, having the same love, being in full accord and of one mind. Do nothing from rivalry or conceit, but in humility count others more significant than yourselves. Let each of you look not only to his own interests, but also to the interests of others. Have this mind among yourselves, which is yours in Christ Jesus, who, though he was in the form of God, did not count equality with God a thing to be grasped, but made himself nothing, taking the form of a servant, being born in the likeness of men. And being found in human form, he humbled himself by becoming obedient to the point of death, even death on a cross. Therefore God has highly exalted him and bestowed on him the name that is above every name, so that at the name of Jesus every knee should bow, in heaven and on earth and under the earth, and every tongue confess that Jesus Christ is Lord.

Do you recognize the omission? Let's look at verses 9–11 again and emphasize the last part of verse 11:

> Therefore God has highly exalted him and bestowed on him the name that is above every name, so that at the name of Jesus every knee should bow, in heaven and on earth and under the earth, and every tongue confess that Jesus Christ is Lord, *to the glory of God the Father.*

Jesus was exalted so that one day every tongue will praise his name, *to the glory of God the Father.* Since 1 Corinthians 10:31 tells us to do everything to the glory of God, we can assume Jesus did just that. He didn't regard equality with God as something to be grasped, *to the glory of God the Father.* He made himself nothing, *to the glory of God the Father.* He took on human form and became a man and was obedient to the point of death on the cross, *to the glory of God the Father.* Everything Jesus did was to God's glory.

Look at another result of our salvation, found in John 5:21–23:

> For just as the Father raises the dead and gives them life, even so the Son gives life to whom he is pleased to give it. Moreover, the Father judges no one, but has entrusted all judgment to the Son, that all may honor the Son just as they honor the Father. Whoever does not honor the Son does not honor the Father, who sent him.

When people give their lives to Christ, they honor the Son. And this, in turn, honors the Father. The New Testament Greek word for "honor" is the verb *timao*, which means to set a price on, and by implication to value, honor, or revere. These are all ways of saying "to glorify God."

Remember, in Romans 15:8–9 Paul gives a reason why Christ came: "For I tell you that Christ became a servant to the circumcised to show God's truthfulness, in order to confirm the promises given to the patriarchs, and in order that the Gentiles might glorify God for his mercy" (ESV). We Gentiles (the vast majority of humanity) are saved for a purpose: to glorify God. It gets back to the other side of the cross. Life is all about God and his glory. The more we focus on it, the more we will delight in it. The more we delight in it, the more it shines. The more it shines, the more others will delight in it. And on and on it goes.

To bring God more glory is the reason we are to share our faith with others. Look at 2 Corinthians 4:15: “All this is for your benefit, so that the grace that is reaching more and more people may cause thanksgiving to overflow to the glory of God.”

As we share our faith (grace reaching more and more people), people come to know God. As they come to know God, they give thanks to him for his grace and mercy. As they give thanks, they are giving glory to God. It all goes back to God’s glory, and it brings into focus the other side of the cross.

Yes, Christ died for us, and he died to bring glory to the Father. Never get them out of priority. One is subservient to the other. In dying for us, Christ was reaching his highest goal: bringing glory to his Father.

“But why can’t they at least be equal?” cries the cat Christian focused solely on the first side of the cross. Keep reading!

CHAPTER 14

Can They Be Equal?

Primary writer: Bob

Some of you might feel that we haven't completely answered the question of whether Christ's death could be equally for our sins and for the Father's glory. Others might believe that the Scriptures we have pointed out so far have answered the question, even if indirectly. For those of you in the first category, we are going to attempt to answer the question once and for all.

There are two possible ways that Christ, theoretically, could have died equally for his Father's glory and for us. The first is that Jesus himself chose to die equally for both. The second is that God the Father told Jesus to die equally for both.

Let's consider the first option. Could Christ have gone to the cross thinking, *Hmm, I love both humanity and my Father equally; therefore, I'm going to die for both equally*? We say no. Why? Because this would violate the principle found in Luke 16:13: "No one can serve two masters. Either you will hate the one and love the other, or you will be devoted to the one and despise the other. You cannot serve both God and money."

Though Jesus' words here are in the context of loving money, the principle is the same. You cannot love God equally with anyone or anything else. This is why the Lord said, in the first of the Ten Commandments, "You shall have no other gods before me" (Exodus 20:3).

For Christ to love us and his Father equally would put us at the same level as his holy, holy, holy Father. Sinful, rebellious creatures on the same level as the Almighty? That can't be correct.

That scenario would also contradict what Jesus taught in Matthew 10:37: "Anyone who loves their father or mother more than me is not worthy of me; anyone who loves their son or daughter more than me is not worthy of me." Although Jesus wouldn't technically love us "more than" his Father, putting us on the same level comes dangerously close. It just wouldn't make sense. How could Christ love us equally to the Father? He couldn't.

How about the second option? What if God the Father basically said to God the Son, "Obey me by dying equally for them and for my glory"? If that was the case, it was the Father's decision, not Christ's.

Would this situation violate any Scripture? Yes. In the introduction to this book we stated that whatever we claim to learn in the Bible must apply everywhere in the Bible. With that in mind, note what the Lord said to the people of Israel in Ezekiel 36 when they repeatedly disobeyed him in the Promised Land:

> Again the word of the LORD came to me: "Son of man, when the people of Israel were living in their own land, they defiled it by their conduct and their actions. Their conduct was like a woman's monthly uncleanness in my sight. So I poured out my wrath on them because they had shed blood in the land and because they had defiled it with their idols. I dispersed them among the nations, and they were scattered through the countries; I judged them according to their conduct and their actions. And wherever they went among the nations they profaned my holy name, for it was said of them, 'These are the LORD's people, and yet they had to leave his land.' *I had concern for my holy name*, which the people of Israel profaned among the nations where they had gone."
>
> Ezekiel 36:16–21 (emphasis added)

What do you sense God is concerned about at this point? His holy name is the clear answer. That's because the nations were basically saying, "Their God isn't powerful enough to keep them in their Promised Land. That's not the kind of God I want to worship." God is concerned first and foremost about his reputation. Why? So others can worship him. Why? So they can have the greatest joy.

So what did God do? He brought the Israelites back home. Why? Because he loved them so much and because they were such precious, wonderful people? No. In the next verses we read these words:

> Therefore say to the Israelites, "This is what the Sovereign LORD says: *It is not for your sake, people of Israel, that I am going to do these things, but for the sake of my holy name*, which you have profaned among the nations where you have gone. I will show the holiness of my great name, which has been profaned among the nations, the name you have profaned among them. Then the nations will know that I am the LORD, declares the Sovereign LORD, *when I am proved holy through you before their eyes*."
>
> Ezekiel 36:22–23 (emphasis added)

God made it very clear that he did everything for his name's sake, not for the sake of his people. It wasn't about them, nor is it about us. It was about his holy name. He took action so that as many people as possible (the nations) would take notice and say, "I want to know that powerful God."

As we see in the last words of verse 23, the Lord was proving his holiness through the Israelites before the eyes of the nations. It wasn't primarily about the people of Israel. It was primarily about the Father's glory. Likewise, Jesus didn't say in John 12, "Father, save these kind, wonderful, worthy people from hell. They don't deserve it."

If God the Father lives for the sake of his great and holy name, why would he command his Son to live equally for us and for his glory? The only conclusion we can draw is that he wouldn't. Christ's dying for us and for his Father's glory were not equal. One was greater than the other, and Jesus' death for the Father's glory wins since it is consistent with the rest of Scripture.

Pause a second and take a deep breath. Now let's change gears slightly.

If it's not about us, why are there so many Scriptures that seem to say just the opposite, such as "I came that they may have life and have it abundantly" (John 10:10, ESV)? An abundant life? That sounds like it's about us. Or how about "Whoever believes in me, as the Scripture has said, 'Out of his heart will flow rivers of living water'" (John 7:38, ESV)? That sounds like it's about us too.

We have repeatedly addressed the question about the Scriptures seeming to point to us. But if it hasn't clicked, let me address the question again. The reason why many Scriptures seem to say that it's about us is simple. When we focus on God's glory, declaring that everything is all about him and that he is our greatest treasure and prize, our joy will be at its fullest. Out of our innermost being will flow rivers of living water, and our life will be full and abundant.

If we say, however, that it's equally about us and God, we are on very tricky theological ground. At times we will have great joy (focusing on God), while at other times we will not (focusing on us). It's the difference between saying, "I'm pursuing my greatest joy by pursuing God," versus "I'm pursuing God, and that will result in my greatest joy." Notice which comes first in each statement: God or us. The first statement can be risky. The second is a guarantee.

When I speak to groups about this subject, I compare this concept to bowling. Seeking your joy by pursuing God, like cat Christians who desire God but are primarily interested in what he gives them, is like bowling on a convex alley—where the middle of the alley is higher than the two sides and the gutters. Rolling your ball perfectly straight and keeping it on the top of the ridge in order to hit the headpin is extremely tough, though it can be done.

Pursuing God and expecting joy as a result, like a dog Christian, is like bowling on a concave alley—where the middle of the alley is lower than the two sides and the gutters. Even if you are a little off, the ball is going to roll back into the middle, and you are well ensured of hitting the headpin.

You may be complaining, "This book has made it into an either/or question about God or us. That's not right. It's both—God and us." We would contend that you're wrong if you're saying this with the mindset that Christ died equally for us and for the Father's glory. But if you're saying, "It's both—God and us," with the mindset that Christ died *primarily* for the Father's glory, you are correct.

Quoting John Piper again, "God is most glorified in us when we are most satisfied in him." Pursuing God and his glory first and foremost will bring us our greatest joy.

CHAPTER 15
Evangelical Humanists

Primary writer: Kevin

It's interesting how easily something that is good can rob us of that which is best. Take humanism, for example. In its proper definition, humanism is "any system or mode of thought or action in which human interests, values, and dignity predominate."[1] In other words, people's needs are the highest priority.

Jesus spoke about people's needs. He spoke about feeding the hungry, giving a drink of water to the thirsty, welcoming strangers, clothing the naked, taking care of the sick, and visiting people in prison (Matthew 25:31–46). Jesus spoke highly about meeting the needs of people, although he never said that those needs should "predominate."

Many young people in the church today are focused on obeying those commands of Jesus. They go out on their own and feed the homeless. They carry around signs in busy streets that offer "Free Hugs."[2] They go to prisons and work in orphanages. They travel to countries ravaged by tsunamis and give months of their lives to help the victims. They are helping people, and God is pleased.

Can there come a point, however, where the needs of people become a higher priority in our lives than the glory of God? Yes. Why is this? In part because humanism has influenced not only our culture but the church as well. It has caused, within evangelical circles, something that DeVern Fromke, in his book *Unto Full Stature*, calls "evangelical humanism."[3]

Evangelical humanism basically says, "The chief end of Christianity is to make people happy after they die." In other words, life is all about saving people from hell. Saving people becomes a higher priority than God himself.

Some of you may be ready to put this book down, wondering, "How in the world can saving people from hell, which is so good, become a higher priority than glorifying God? Saving people from hell *does* glorify God."

Indeed it does. We know that clearly from Scripture. But for many of us in the church, unfortunately, saving souls can become *all* there is to the Christian life. Saving people from hell *becomes an end in and of itself.*

When I was in college, I was privileged to be heavily involved in a campus ministry. It formed a great foundation for my Christian life, as I was taught the importance of quiet times, Bible study, prayer, fellowship, and evangelism. I was taught to share my faith, to overcome objections, and hopefully to ultimately lead someone to pray to receive Christ.

Part of my discipleship was to share my faith with a certain number of students at our campus each week. In addition to that, I went on summer projects and spring break projects where much of the activity was centered on sharing our faith and hopefully seeing people come to Christ. These were all very good things. Without even realizing it, however, saving people from hell was becoming the goal of my Christian life. It was basically how I kept score of my success as a Christian. Slowly growing on my shoulders was a tremendous weight to be successful through winning souls.

Several years after graduating from college and leaving that ministry, I realized I had gotten to the point where I very rarely shared my faith with Americans. I took the occasional mission trip with my church and participated in evangelism, but for the most part I really didn't share my faith with friends, neighbors, or coworkers. I didn't find joy in the Christian life. In fact, most of the time I felt guilty.

When I sat back and considered why this was the case, I realized that what I had come to know in my collegiate Christian life wasn't all that fulfilling. Frankly, I really wasn't excited about sharing with other people about how they too could become a Christian, be guaranteed eternal life, then get trained in the art of evangelism, and have this tremendous weight of responsibility on their shoulders. Did I really want to invite them to a life of guilt? Did I really want them to become like me, spending the rest of their lives worrying about all the nonbelievers who were going to die and go to hell unless they got going and tried to get them to pray to become a Christian?

What I realize now is that *most of my Christian life centered on avoiding guilt*. I had never found the treasure of just knowing Jesus. My treasure was getting others to know him, while never knowing and enjoying him myself. Saving lost people had become a higher priority than God.

Without knowing it, I had been unintentionally trained in college to be an evangelical humanist. The problem with being an evangelical humanist is that you are basically saying people are the most important thing in the Christian life, and saving people from hell takes priority over everything else.

As a result, I was motivated to do evangelism through guilt rather than through joy. We were challenged to become missionaries through guilt: "You don't want all those people to go to hell, do you?" Those going into pastoral ministry were challenged to see how many baptisms they could have each month (i.e., how many people were saved from hell). Everything revolved around saving people from hell.

We like to say that there are four deaths we need to die to as Christians. We need to die to ourselves. We are all familiar with that. We also need to die to our family and friends. Most are familiar with that. On top of that we need to die to our national heritage and pride. (Is it "God bless America" or "America bless God"?) Few people are aware of that. What even fewer realize, however, is that we need to die to humanity. Humankind—people—cannot be the center of our attention.

A focus on saving people from hell, which is so good, can bring tragic results when it becomes our treasure. We see pastors who are aggressively sharing their faith but whose marriages and families are falling apart. They lead the church, but their personal walk with the Lord is anemic. Unfortunately, no one in the church can approach them about these issues because the pastors are successfully sharing Jesus with people. You never dare challenge an evangelical humanist. After all, they are doing so much good—saving so many people from hell.

This tragedy can be observed in missionaries as well. Too often we have seen missionaries come home from the field and end up getting divorced. Why? Because they became so focused on planting churches that they forgot to show the glory of God in their own marriages and families. One missionary child stated, "I wish I'd been a Muslim. My father would have spent more time with me."

But if you know there are two sides to the cross, and, unlike a cat Christian, you understand that the cross is not just about saving people from hell, you can challenge evangelical humanism. Why? Life is not *solely* about saving people from hell. It is about the glory of God in *every* area of life.

In Matthew 13:44, Jesus taught a striking little parable about the value of being a member of his kingdom: "The kingdom of heaven is like treasure hidden in a field. When a man found it, he hid it again, and then in his joy went and sold all he had and bought that field." Though Bob and I interpret this parable as speaking primarily of God treasuring us, it is also safe to say that we are to treasure God. When people see that we have something so valuable—Christ as our treasure—that we are willing to give up everything for it, they will come running to find out what that is. Everyone is seeking that kind of joy.

We hope this is helping you see that when we look only at the cat's side of the cross we are not only in danger of believing that life is about us, but we might become evangelical humanists, living like life is all about people. When this happens, Christ is no longer our treasure. People are.

If we live for ourselves, we live for everything that will make us happy: our families, our careers, etc. If we live for humanity, we live for everything that will make people happy—first and foremost to be saved from hell. In either case, Jesus has been displaced, God's glory has been cast aside, and the ultimate result will be a bitter, burned-out Christian life.

Let me give you an example from my own life of how I avoided this.

A few years ago I had the privilege of being the CEO of a church-planting organization in a closed country. This group had targeted a very remote area of the world, an area with harsh conditions and many challenges. Seven churches had come together to endeavor to plant a church among this totally unreached people. This effort was born from the vision of three families that had been on the field and saw a unique opportunity to be part of revealing God's glory to these people. These families braved harsh conditions, a hostile government, and a resistant people. They persevered greatly to reach this people group.

When I became a leader in the organization, the project had been in existence for five years. I had the responsibility of communicating to the churches what was involved in this task, raising funds, and recruiting new workers. My first step was to visit the team overseas, assess the work being done, and encourage them in this difficult task.

At this point in my life I had come to realize there was more than just one side to the cross. As a result, I knew this project was about more than seeing a church planted among an unreached people group. It was about the glory of God being revealed in every aspect of the project: in the lives and families of everyone involved, in the churches that had chosen to partner in this endeavor, and in how we were perceived by the government in the country.

Because of this, whenever I spoke about the project—whether at board meetings, to the staff, or to the churches—I was careful to define the goal as glorifying God by *endeavoring* to plant a church in a God-honoring way.

Why was I so careful to do that? I knew we couldn't define success by whether or not we planted a church among that unreached people group. In reality, that work was up to God. If he chose to do it through our group—fantastic! What a privilege! But if God chose to do it another way, that was his prerogative. If planting a church had been our primary goal, we would have failed if God chose not to do it through us.

That project is still in existence today. The endeavor to plant a church among that people group goes on, but has yet to be accomplished. Meanwhile I am no longer the leader of the U.S. side of that ministry, and the three founding families have left the effort. One family left after the death of a child, another left because of the illness of one of its children, and the third family moved on after many years of difficult, self-sacrificing service with many highs and lows.

Had our goal been solely to win souls and plant a church, we all would have been failures. But because our goal was to glorify God by *endeavoring* to plant a church, all three families and I were successful. I believe we all glorified God through our act of worship as we endeavored to plant a church in that area.

We hope you can see how focusing on the other side of the cross frees evangelical humanists—especially on the missionary field.

When these families were forced to come home because of circumstances outside of their control, they came home knowing they had glorified God. Had they been evangelical humanists, they would have cried, "God, whose side are you on? We gave our lives to reach these people, and you're forcing us to leave without seeing nearly as many souls won as we had dreamed. And what about planting a church? What are you doing?" It would have been easy for them to get angry and bitter with God, and they could have potentially lost their entire walk with the Lord.

Yet because they saw the other side of the cross, they were free to say, "OK, Lord, I don't understand. But if you want us to glorify you back where we came from, so be it. We can glorify you there just as much as we can glorify you here." They were, and still are, free.

Freedom is found in living for the glory of God more than anything else.

CHAPTER 16
A Christian Cancer

Primary writer: Bob

When cat Christians focus primarily on the "me" side of the cross, we will say it again, their theology is not incorrect. Jesus did die for them. He did think of them on the cross. He does love them. He does want to bless them. This is all correct. Their theology, however, is incomplete. There is the other side, which says that life is primarily about God and his glory.

If you never learn about the other side of the cross, but instead keep your focus solely on the cat's perspective, your Christianity can become like aspirin. As we pointed out earlier, aspirin taken in small doses can take away a headache or other aches and pains, but if you overdose on it, it can kill you. That is what happened to John and Debbie, the imaginary couple we followed in chapter 3.

This is a warning to those who know only the cat's side of the cross. Overdosing on what Jesus did for us can kill us, because it puts the focus on us and *we become more important than God's glory.*

There are many passages in the New Testament that help us place humanity in the proper perspective. Let's start with the sixth chapter of John's Gospel. The chapter begins with Jesus feeding five thousand men (plus women and children). This multitude consisted of Jews, people excited about the possibility of having the Messiah come to free them from Roman oppression. That evening Jesus and his disciples crossed the Sea of Galilee and went to Capernaum. The next morning the people couldn't find Jesus, so they went looking for him.

Why? What was their motivation? *The Message* puts it well, noting that Jesus said, "You've come looking for me not because you saw God in my actions but because I fed you, filled your stomachs—and for free" (John 6:26).

What were these people doing? They were seeking God for what they could get from him, not for who he is. Like the older brother in the parable of the prodigal son, they weren't interested in a relationship—they were only interested in a reward. Like John and Debbie, they wanted to get things from God.

Continuing to focus on the cat's side of the cross will prohibit you from serving God with all your heart. It will cause you to avoid anything that has to do with suffering or sacrificing for God's glory, and it will cause you to keep targeting a safe, happy, comfortable life. That is what is happening in the church today. And it is nothing new; it was happening when the New Testament was being written.

In his letter to the Galatians, Paul tried to inform the believers in Galatia that they didn't need to be circumcised as others were telling them they needed to be. He explained that if they did so they would have to keep the entire law and that Christ would be "of no value" to them (Galatians 5:2–3).

Near the end of the letter, Paul described the motivation of those who wanted the Galatians to be circumcised: "Those who want to impress people by means of the flesh are trying to compel you to be circumcised. The only reason they do this is to avoid being persecuted for the cross of Christ" (Galatians 6:12).

These Judaizers, as they are often called, really weren't concerned about living for the glory of God—certainly not to the point of suffering. That's because they didn't actually have a relationship with the Lord. They just wanted to look like they did. They went to the synagogues, paid their tithes, and offered their sacrifices, but deep in their hearts they were concerned only about themselves. They did everything they could to protect their safe, happy, and comfortable lives. And they were finding that living for Christ meant persecution, so they wanted to revert back to Judaism.

As a missions mobilizer, it's easy for me to spot this Galatians 6:12 attitude. When I speak about God's global glory and challenge audiences to consider going overseas, many people shut down emotionally since the thought of going overseas scares them to death. Why? They would have to suffer. It would mean leaving their safe, happy, comfortable life, and that is the very thing they live for. Why do something totally against what you live for, and suffer instead? That's ridiculous.

They are living for themselves in a Christian context because they have focused only on the cat's side of the cross. That is the most obvious danger of this focus. There are other dangers as well, however.

Paul's words to Timothy in 2 Timothy 2:15 provide us with a basic message that God has for each of us: "Do your best to present yourself to God as one approved, a worker who has no need to be ashamed, *rightly handling* the word of truth" (ESV, emphasis added). The Greek word for "rightly handling" literally translates as "making a straight cut." Our doctrine needs to be straight and pure.

Now look at Acts 20:29–30, part of Paul's emotional message to the elders of the church at Ephesus in light of the fact that he believed he wouldn't see them again: "I know that after my departure fierce wolves will come in among you, not sparing the flock; and from among your own selves will arise men speaking *twisted things*, to draw away the disciples after them" (ESV, emphasis added). The Greek word for "twisted things" has the sense of "making crooked."

Note the different motivations in these two passages. We're told in 2 Timothy 2:15 to make things straight. The false teachers Paul warned about in Acts 20:30, on the other hand, would make things crooked.

Those who heed 2 Timothy 2:15 will present themselves to God as having correctly handled God's Word. They live for God.

It's all about God; it's not about them. But the false teachers will "draw away the disciples *after them.*" What does that mean? They will preach the gospel *in order to get followers.* In other words, they don't want a small church—they want a *big* church. They want *lots* of people. It's all about people. God is second. The Lord will still be glorified through the winning of souls, but he is the second priority. Because these people want a big church, they preach a gospel that is more palatable, a gospel that won't offend anyone in any way. This is a crooked doctrine, and it is spreading like cancer in our churches.

This crooked, malignant teaching is a safe, cozy message about God's love and mercy. The leaders of these churches choose songs that people like. Announcements are given in a way that entertains people. If the cross is offensive, take it out of the church. Nowhere does the Bible say you have to have a cross in your church. If some songs are offensive, don't sing them. If a sermon is offensive, don't preach it. Preach messages instead that will make people feel good.

By preaching a crooked doctrine, you create a tumorous religion in which people are primary and God's glory is secondary. Whatever pleases people and draws them into the church is what receives a green light.

Kevin and I believe Joel Osteen is a pastor who fits this category. Does he love God? Only the Lord knows, but we have no reason to believe he does not. Is he saved? We think so. Are his messages right on? Though we believe that many of them are not *incorrect,* we would say that they are *incomplete.* Joel's followers are overdosing on these incomplete messages; and, like too much aspirin, this is going to destroy them.

Joel was interviewed on the TV show *Fox and Friends* (November 4, 2009) as he was kicking off his new book, *It's Your Time: Activate Your Faith, Achieve Your Dreams, and Increase in God's Favor.*[1] The program aired during the time when President Obama was ending his first year as president and the unemployment rate was just below

10 percent. In his book, Joel makes a parallel between birthing a child and coming through hard times.

In the *Fox and Friends* interview, Joel said, "It's always the most difficult before you're about to give birth. And so you have to stay determined. You have to realize, right past the pain, right past the discouragement, is another great victory. . . . Life is like that—giving birth to our dreams."

After Steve Doocy commented that our best days could still be before us, Joel replied, "You know, that's what we believe. Seasons come and seasons go, and I don't believe you'd still be alive if God didn't have another victory in your future. Sometimes you go through a loss or something bad and you think, *My best days are behind me.* But all of us need to hold on to the fact that we have potential in us and we have things that God wants to do great in our future."

Note that everything is geared toward *our* benefit. It's about *our* victory, *our* dreams, *our* best days being ahead of us, great things in *our* future. There is no mention that any of this has to do with God's glory. And if Joel or someone from his staff would say, "Of course it's about God's glory; we just don't put it in those words," we would reply, "Why not? Why is it left out and just assumed?"

Because so much teaching stems from the cat's side of the cross, we can't assume that a teaching or ministry is all about God's glory. That reality must be spelled out explicitly. That's what our book is calling for.

Here's our question: Can Joel's teaching apply to every person? Would it apply to Pastor Manuel of San Jose del Guaviare, Colombia? Were his best days ahead of him six weeks before Joel's interview on *Fox and Friends*? We don't think it would apply, since on September 21, 2009, Pastor Manuel was martyred for preaching Christ.[2]

Are the best days ahead for Pastor Manuel's wife? Without her husband and raising her young children alone, she has a tough road ahead of her. But Pastor Manuel's death brought great glory to God.

And his wife's life will bring great glory to God as she leans on him for her day-to-day survival.

If you are focused on God's glory, then the glory theme works here. If you are focused on the "best days ahead of us" theme, that theme falls short.

It's really not a question of whether Joel Osteen's church is biblical or unbiblical. The real question is whether Joel's church is painting the full picture or overdosing on one side of the cross, by focusing on itself and enjoying God's blessings—not God himself.

Does this mean that the best days are *not* ahead of us, and therefore what Joel is preaching is wrong? No, not necessarily. Remember, his preaching is not incorrect, but incomplete. For some of us, our best days (in terms of things like finances and significance) surely are ahead, and those best days will bring God great glory. God may ask others of us, however, to suffer—even to be martyrs—in order to glorify his name. In the world's eyes, those aren't the "best days ahead." But from a dog's point of view, they are!

Rather than being fixed on our best days ahead (as the world would see it), we need to be looking for God's glory shining in our lives. Which of the two motivations has our primary attention? The answer to that question depends upon which side of the cross we are focusing on.

Don't forget what we wrote in the introduction. If a teaching can't apply to each and every person in each and every circumstance in his or her life, then that theology is lacking.

When you focus only on the cat's perspective of the cross, you can produce a very enticing message; so of course many people will want to come and hear you. The leaders of megachurches will say, "Look how God is blessing our church!" Those who have seen the other side of the cross, meanwhile, will say, "Your message is self-centered and therefore understandably attracting people. It's not incorrect; it's just incomplete."

It's so easy to overdose on the cat's side of the cross; and without realizing it, all you do and say can be counterproductive to the kingdom of God. This is a danger the seeker-sensitive church movement faces. It's easy to make lost people a higher priority than God's glory (though members of the movement will say they reach the lost for God's glory). And everything then revolves around people, not God. If people want videos, the seeker-sensitive folks use videos. If people want contemporary songs, they sing them. Whatever the people want, they give it to them.

A friend of mine recently asked me to look at the website of the church he is attending. Here are the pastor's opening words: "At our church, we value people because that's what's important to God. Thus we focus on meeting the needs of people." Right off the bat this pastor put people on center stage, reflecting a cat-meology. There was no mention of God's glory.

Now let us be very clear here. Videos, contemporary songs, and sanctuaries without crosses *are not wrong at all.* There is nothing wrong with attracting people to the church in a people-centered fashion. What is wrong is teaching biblical messages from only one side of the cross and totally abandoning the idea that life is first and foremost about God and his glory.

It's wrong to teach a gospel that applies only to certain times in our lives but not to other times. If your message applies only to an American with an externally blessed life and not to a Chinese pastor who has been in prison for twenty-two years, you have no message.

When we lose sight of God's glory, we have lost everything. We will struggle as we live out a dry, lifeless Christianity, not fully understanding what life is about. We will apply certain passages at certain times and other passages at other times, seeking that safe, happy, comfortable life. In the end, we won't be free because we are too focused on ourselves.

Too many Christians are focused on the cat's side of the cross. As a result, you can't tell the difference between the typical Christian and the typical non-Christian in America. They are both working toward the same goals. They are both living for the American dream. Their lifestyles are almost exactly the same, except one swears and goes to bars while the other says, "Praise the Lord," and goes to church. Besides that, they both live the same kind of lifestyle.

It is interesting to examine how numbers oriented, or seeker sensitive, Jesus was in his ministry. The fact is, he was not numbers oriented. Although he came to seek and save the lost, he wasn't concerned about the number of people who followed him. It wasn't about them; it was about glorifying God.

We can see this as we return to John 6. Jesus gave the crowd following him a difficult-to-understand lesson on what it would mean to spend eternity with him. He spoke of being the "bread of life" and about their need to drink his blood and eat his flesh (vv. 51–58).

Realizing that Jesus' teaching was hard, his disciples said, "This is a hard teaching. Who can accept it?" (v. 60). The disciples were worried about people. They assumed Jesus was about a political kingdom that would overthrow Roman rule; hence, they needed lots of people to fight.

After giving his disciples a slight rebuke, we see Jesus do something amazing in verses 66 and 67: "From this time many of his disciples turned back and no longer followed him. 'You do not want to leave too, do you?' Jesus asked the Twelve."

The first amazing thing is what Jesus did *not* do. Jesus did *not* run after the disciples who turned away from him. He did *not* yell, "Wait! I know what I said was offensive, but I didn't mean that you literally have to drink my blood and eat my flesh. That was an analogy. All you have to do is believe in me and eat some bread and drink some wine. That won't be too hard, will it?"

No. Jesus let them go. He wasn't worried about numbers or about offending people.

But notice that Jesus did something even more amazing. After watching many people leave, he even challenged his inner circle of twelve disciples to see if they wanted to leave. Talk about not being into numbers!

Jesus was willing to offend anyone and everyone with the truth, even if they didn't understand it. Why? Because the glory of his Father was first and foremost in his mind. Whatever the Father would do by the moving of the Holy Spirit was up to him. Jesus would simply preach the truth and see what God was doing. Jesus was into obedience, not numbers.

One Sunday, Pastor Rob Rhoden told our congregation a fitting story about his recent vacation. While they were at the pool, his young son Miles announced to all his cousins, "I'm going to do a cannonball—and I'm going to make a big splash." Rob and his wife looked at each other in amazement because they knew their little son hated to get into water.

Sure enough, their nieces and nephews had a great time in the pool while Miles ran around the perimeter of the pool, yelling things like "Throw the ball to me!" and "Catch this!" When they all got out and dried themselves off, there was Miles with a towel, drying off even though he had never gotten wet.

Rob and his wife wondered if Miles was afraid of the water because his cousins were wearing swimming gear and he wasn't. The next morning they purchased some swimming paraphernalia—flippers, goggles, and even a snorkeling mouthpiece—thinking it would inspire him to venture into the water.

That afternoon Miles proudly showed up wearing his flippers and goggles, and even sporting the snorkeling mouthpiece in his mouth. What was the result? He ran all around the perimeter of the pool, never once taking off his goggles, flippers, or mouthpiece.

As Rob watched this scene, a thought occurred to him. "This is what we are doing in the church," he told us that Sunday. "We are preparing people for ministry, but so few are actually getting into the water." We say we are living for God's glory as we run around the outside of the pool yelling, "It's all about God." But in actuality we are living for ourselves.

This is something we must avoid, and it can be avoided—by looking at the other side of the cross and preaching a "straight doctrine." When we place God's glory in its rightful position, everything falls into place; and our message will apply to all people in whatever circumstances they find themselves.

CHAPTER 17

To Suffer or Not to Suffer

Primary writer: Bob

When my daughters were young, the "happening" thing for little girls was Build-A-Bear. If you aren't familiar with this concept, you take your child to the Build-A-Bear store and allow her not only to purchase a furry little friend but also to stuff it and accessorize it with clothes, shoes, sports gear, electronics, furniture . . . you name it, and you can probably buy it!

The idea is to purchase and customize your own personal teddy bear. This reminds me of what many Christians have done with God. They want a "Build-A-God." Their desire is to worship a God who will bring them pleasure. As a result, they look at the options that come with God—joy, gladness, suffering, struggles, testing, etc.—and say, "I'd like a God who gives me joy and gladness, but I'll leave the suffering, struggles, and testing parts out. That won't be the God I worship, because that wouldn't make me feel good."

This is the epitome of looking at the cross only through a cat's eyes. We tailor God to fit our needs and wishes.

The conclusions that can be drawn from the two sides of the cross are very, very different. We discussed this in chapters 1 and 2. When a person is focused solely on the cat's side of the cross, he prays, "Jesus, thank you for dying on the cross for me." That isn't incorrect, but it's focused only on one side of the cross. Those who know both sides of the cross also thank Jesus for dying for them. But they add to that something like, "Jesus, thank you for dying on the cross for me in order to reveal the Father's glory."

Those few extra words change everything. The first person concludes that since Jesus suffered and died for him, he is not going to suffer. How does he reach that conclusion? He reasons, "Since Jesus left the Father's glory, came to the earth, and suffered and died for me, that's a pretty good sign that it's all about me. And now that he's gone back to heaven and is preparing a mansion for me, he must live for me. This is great! Because there is no more death or mourning or crying or pain in heaven (that is, no suffering—Revelation 21:4), *and* because Jesus suffered and died for me here on the earth, he must not want suffering to be a part of my life at all. Therefore I don't have to suffer; he did it all for me. Yes! I guess that's what they mean when they talk about Jesus' *substitutionary* death!"

Those who have seen the other side of the cross conclude something very different: "Since Jesus suffered and died for me in order to reveal the Father's glory, he has given me an example that I should be willing to suffer in order to reveal that same glory." They realize that it is *primarily* about the glory of the Father. They believe that whatever makes the glory of the Father shine is what must be done. If it means suffering, then so be it. God's glory is worthy of our lives, our suffering, and even our martyrdom.

In simple terms, dog Christians—believers who have embraced the other side of the cross—are willing to suffer. Cat Christians—believers who have seen only one side of the cross—are not.

Are there any passages of Scripture that support the idea that we should be willing to suffer? Absolutely! In 1 Peter 2:13–17, Peter wrote about showing respect and submitting to authority. Then he turned to specifically address slaves:

> Slaves, in reverent fear of God submit yourselves to your masters, not only to those who are good and considerate, but also to those who are harsh. For it is

> commendable if someone bears up under the pain of unjust suffering because they are conscious of God. But how is it to your credit if you receive a beating for doing wrong and endure it? But if you suffer for doing good and you endure it, this is commendable before God. To this you were called, because *Christ suffered for you, leaving you an example, that you should follow in his steps.*
>
> 1 Peter 2:18–21 (emphasis added)

"What?" cries a cat Christian. "I've been called to suffer? That's not what I signed up for. And why would Jesus want me to suffer if he died for me and suffered in my behalf so that I wouldn't have to suffer?"

To someone who espouses cat-meology, this passage is incomprehensible. Dog Christians, however, find it is easy to understand. They see that Christ suffered primarily to reveal the Father's glory. Therefore they should be willing to suffer too. The text makes perfect sense.

Need more evidence? Look at Paul's totally un-American theology as he wrote to the Philippians about spreading the gospel and standing strong on it: "It has been granted to you that for the sake of Christ you should not only believe in him *but also suffer for his sake*" (Philippians 1:29, ESV, emphasis added).

The word "granted" is translated from the Greek word *charizomai*, which means "to give freely, or graciously, as a favor." In other words, not only did God do something pleasant in your behalf to get you to believe in him, but he also did you a favor by allowing you to suffer for him.

Note also the phrase "for his sake." God doesn't delight in suffering just for the sake of suffering. He knows that is crazy. Why is suffering for Christ's sake different? Because of what it does for us (we'll discuss that in chapter 19, "The Personal Benefits of Suffering") and because he rewards those who suffer for his sake. The rewards far outweigh the suffering. We see that in Romans 8:18: "I consider that our present sufferings are not worth comparing with the glory that will be revealed in us."

When you look at it from an eternal perspective, the sufferings we may experience in this life are nothing compared to what we receive for eternity. The suffering we experience here on this earth, therefore, is a blessing. It has been *granted* to us to suffer.

Paul not only spoke of suffering as a gift, but he went even further when he wrote to Timothy. He actually encouraged Timothy to come alongside him and suffer: "So do not be ashamed of the testimony about our Lord or of me his prisoner. Rather, *join with me in suffering for the gospel*, by the power of God" (2 Timothy 1:8, emphasis added). Paul was asking Timothy, as well as you and me, to join him in suffering for the gospel.

Suffering is a definite theme in 1 Peter, as we see in 1 Peter 4:1: "Therefore, since Christ suffered in his body, arm yourselves also with the same attitude."

When cat Christians read verses like these, they have to deal with the reality that suffering is clearly affirmed in the Scriptures. How do they allow for this in their theological grid? They will say something like, "OK, so God wants me to suffer. I guess when I'm old, God may give me cancer, and then I'll suffer a few months before I die. I guess that is how God is going to let me suffer."

Dog Christians, by contrast, look at these verses and say, "No way! That is not at all what the Scriptures are saying. God is telling us we should be willing to suffer in any way for his glory because it is worth suffering for. And when we suffer for God's glory, we are racking up glory in heaven that will far outweigh all our suffering."

Now here is how this theology of suffering applies in the Christian life today. When a challenge is given to a church to do something difficult (maybe it means going overseas to take the gospel to Muslims who have never heard it, or ministering to the poor in the inner city, or going to a prison and loving those who are forgotten by our society), a me-centered cat Christian thinks about it for a minute and determines, *That's not going to fit into my goal of having a safe, happy, comfortable life.* A cat quickly concludes, *That can't be God's will for my life. It must be God's plan for someone else in the church.*

A glory-focused dog Christian, on the other hand, thinks, *Wow! This is going to be challenging. But since Jesus suffered and died in order to reveal the Father's glory, I should be willing to suffer as well. I need to seriously consider this challenge to live out my faith.*

Dog Christians don't *seek* suffering, but neither do they shy away from it. Cat Christians, however, run as far away from it as they can. They hate suffering and avoid it at all costs, even at the cost of their eternal rewards.

One time after I spoke on this subject, a woman approached me and said, "Thank you so much for your message on suffering. I have made some decisions in my life that have led to suffering, and it is hurting me tremendously. All of my friends say, 'Why not get out of it? Why do you have to keep suffering?'—as if suffering is wrong. It's hard enough to suffer, but it's even harder when your fellow brothers and sisters in Christ don't believe it is right to suffer. Your message has set me free to realize that what I'm doing is right. Suffering is a part of the Christian life, and it's OK to be in it."

After hearing this message, another woman shared, "When my leg started hurting real bad, and the doctors couldn't do anything, I had people calling me asking if they could come to my home and cast out the devil in the name of Jesus. But I kept saying no. I wanted to see what glory God could get through this first."

Don't avoid suffering, and don't encourage others to avoid it either. Look at the other side of the cross, and realize that everything is about the Father's glory. Then be willing to live, suffer, and possibly die for that glory.

CHAPTER 18

Different Levels of Suffering

Primary writer: Bob

I have found that when I speak about suffering, people feel free to share with me about the suffering they are going through and the thoughts they have on the topic. At one seminar, an American woman who had traveled around the world came up to me and shared, "People from other nations ask us Americans, 'How are you suffering?' When they hear that we aren't suffering, they say, 'We'll pray for you. Because if you're not suffering, something is wrong in your Christianity.'"

Her words made me feel guilty. How could I address the topic of suffering when I wasn't undergoing hardships like so many people throughout the world? I'm not unwilling to suffer, but that simply isn't my circumstance.

I have learned of the immense suffering of fellow believers around the globe in two key ways. First, because I have traveled the world, I know what our brothers and sisters in Christ are going through. When the Southern Baptists asked me to speak at their clusters in West Africa back in 1999, I took my entire family with me in order to expose them to life outside the United States. We met people who had just gone through the Liberian civil war and had absolutely nothing. My wife, Debby, prayed with women who had no idea how they were going to feed their children that day. We saw children running around naked because they had no clothing to wear.

In 2002 our family took the message of "Cat and Dog Theology" to Asia. We spent a month in Bandung, Indonesia, visiting the poorer parts of the city. We shared with families that lived in shacks and had virtually no possessions.

Our American family has known no suffering at all compared to the people we have seen.

My second significant exposure to suffering came from *Foxe's Book of Martyrs*.[1] I read it only once, but I have vivid memories of learning about people being sown up in leather bags with poisonous snakes and thrown into rivers simply because they were Christians. I remember reading of women who were stripped naked in front of crowds, covered in boiling tar, and set on fire simply because they claimed to follow Christ. I remember stories about believers who were put in large pieces of wax and set on fire in order to light Nero's parties.

After reading these stories, I promised the Lord I would never complain about my circumstances again! I had never experienced anything close to the suffering of these brothers and sisters in Christ. And how could I relate to, much less speak about, the passages regarding suffering found in Scripture?

With all of this self-doubt following me, the more I read about suffering and spoke about being willing to suffer, the more powerless I felt. How could I keep speaking on this topic? Then one day I came across two Scripture passages, both written by the apostle Paul, that really helped me understand God's perspective on suffering.

In 2 Corinthians 6, Paul wrote about not putting a stumbling block in anyone's way lest his ministry be hindered. Read what he said, focusing on how he suffered in various ways:

> We put no obstacle in anyone's way, so that no fault may be found with our ministry, but as servants of God we commend ourselves in every way: by great endurance, in afflictions, hardships, calamities, beatings, imprisonments, riots, labors, sleepless nights, hunger; by purity, knowledge, patience, kindness, the Holy Spirit, genuine love; by truthful speech, and the power of God; with the weapons of righteousness for the right hand and for

> the left; through honor and dishonor, through slander and praise. We are treated as impostors, and yet are true; as unknown, and yet well known; as dying, and behold, we live; as punished, and yet not killed; as sorrowful, yet always rejoicing; as poor, yet making many rich; as having nothing, yet possessing everything.
>
> 2 Corinthians 6:3–10, ESV

In 2 Corinthians 11, Paul continued to describe his suffering as an apostle. Look at the list he gave:

> Are they servants of Christ? (I am out of my mind to talk like this.) I am more. I have worked much harder, been in prison more frequently, been flogged more severely, and been exposed to death again and again. Five times I received from the Jews the forty lashes minus one. Three times I was beaten with rods, once I was pelted with stones, three times I was shipwrecked, I spent a night and a day in the open sea, I have been constantly on the move. I have been in danger from rivers, in danger from bandits, in danger from my fellow Jews, in danger from Gentiles; in danger in the city, in danger in the country, in danger at sea; and in danger from false believers. I have labored and toiled and have often gone without sleep; I have known hunger and thirst and have often gone without food; I have been cold and naked. Besides everything else, I face daily the pressure of my concern for all the churches.
>
> 2 Corinthians 11:23–28

What can we learn from this? Paul suffered in numerous ways. He certainly suffered physically. Some forms of physical suffering were great; others were light. There were times when he underwent sleepless nights and was hungry (6:5), and times when he was poor (6:10). He took numerous trips to advance the kingdom (11:26). He was in danger from rivers, robbers, Gentiles, and his fellow Jews, as well as from wilderness, sea, and false brothers (11:26). At times he was without food, water, or shelter and was exposed to the cold (11:27–28). He was shipwrecked, adrift at sea for a day (11:25). In his greatest degree of suffering, Paul was imprisoned, beaten numerous times, and stoned for his faith. Many times he was near death (11:23–25).

In addition to the physical suffering he described, Paul encountered many forms of emotional suffering. He suffered from times of dishonor and slander (6:8) and from times of being unknown (6:9) and treated as an impostor (6:8). Then there were times of sorrow (6:10), and there were also times of being patient (6:6). On top of everything else, Paul wrote of being worried daily about how the churches were doing (11:28).

If we were to try to graph Paul's trials from the least suffering at the top to the greatest suffering at the bottom, it would look something like this:

Emotional Suffering

Dishonor/slander
Being unknown
Worrying about the churches
Treated as an impostor
Sleepless nights
Lots of travel

Light Physical Suffering

Being poor
In serious danger
Cold and hungry
Shipwrecked
Adrift at sea
Imprisonment
Beaten many times
Near death

Great Physical Suffering

Dying for his faith
(not recorded in Scripture)

On this gradient scale, I can safely say that I *have* suffered for the kingdom of God—not in the area of "Great Physical Suffering," but in "Light Physical Suffering" and "Emotional Suffering." As a result, my life does reflect the biblical mandate to suffer—though not to the point of being jailed or beaten.

You may have suffered in this way too. Have you had sleepless nights helping the homeless or traveling on a mission trip? Paul says that is suffering. Have you suffered emotionally by counseling fellow believers for hours upon hours to try to help them overcome their struggles? You too have suffered. Have you experienced tough times walking people through reconciliation? Have you exhorted and challenged others, who didn't want to be challenged, to a holy walk with God? You have suffered, according to the apostle Paul.

Suffering is relative, as a friend of mine says. Three years ago, Jim (not his real name) chose to join the staff of a local ministry. But in order to do so he had to leave his $150,000-per-year job, sell his 3,500-square-foot house, and move his family of five into his father's 600-square-foot basement.

Do you want to know what is most amazing? Jim has a fantastic attitude. He beams with joy and excitement. When someone asks him how he's doing, he replies, "We're living by faith, but this is only suffering by Western standards. Compared to the rest of the world, we're living like kings!"

Suffering is relative.

Perhaps you are suffering because of the choices of others. Even though it may be light suffering, you are suffering. Mary Bosley, a dear friend and supporter of ours, put it this way: "Anything that causes hardship in your life as a result of the sin of others is a form of suffering." If this is your situation, God is preparing glory for you that you could never imagine—glory that far outweighs what you are enduring.

Don't focus solely on the cat's side of the cross and say no to suffering, whether that suffering is great or small.

Richard Wurmbrand used to be known as the voice of the underground church because of the suffering he endured in Romania for preaching the gospel. He spent a total of fourteen years in prison, three of those years in solitary confinement.

After Richard was released from prison, one day he took his confirmation class on a field trip. Though it was a Sunday morning, the pastor didn't take the children to a church; he took them to the zoo. Standing before the cage of lions, he told the boys and girls how believers in years past had faced such wild animals because of their faith. He shared how they were killed by the powerful jaws of the lions simply because they loved Christ.

Why would Richard do this? He wanted these young people to be prepared to face great suffering. He knew firsthand that believers have to be prepared for persecution ahead of time. Richard observed, "It is too difficult to prepare yourself for [suffering] when the Communists have put you in prison. . . . Nobody resists who has not renounced the pleasures of life beforehand."[2]

Establish this firmly in your mind now: Life is not about you having a safe, comfortable, happy life. Suffering is meant to be a part of your life, whether that suffering is emotional or physical, light or heavy. If God calls you to great suffering, embrace it—for the glory of God. Don't run from it. You will miss out on something tremendous.

What tremendous thing awaits those who suffer? Keep reading.

CHAPTER 19

The Personal Benefits of Suffering

Primary writer: Kevin

As missions mobilizers, we pick up on certain topics and catchy phrases that others use. One that I use with my audiences—and forgive me, but I've heard it so much that I don't know to whom the credit is due!—goes like this: "If you don't do Acts 1:8, you get Acts 8:1."

In Acts 1:8, the risen Christ said to his disciples, "You will receive power when the Holy Spirit comes on you; and you will be my witnesses in Jerusalem, and in all Judea and Samaria, and to the ends of the earth."

The idea is both/and—*both* Jerusalem *and* Judea *and* Samaria *and* to the ends of the earth. Notice it was not either/or, as if the disciples had a choice, or first/then, as if it is progressive. Wherever you are reading this, you are supposed to be touching your neighbors and the nations.

How did the disciples respond to this both/and commission? Did they immediately go out to the nations? We read in Acts 2:41 that three thousand people were added to their number. By Acts 4:4 that number had grown to five thousand men (plus women and children). The gospel continued to spread like wildfire (see Acts 5:14; 6:7), but only in Jerusalem.

Because the movement was confined to Jerusalem, the Lord used his "involuntary go mechanism" to get the disciples out to the nations. In Acts 7, Stephen was stoned. And after that Saul (later known as Paul) began to persecute the church. This is where suffering comes in. Saul went from house to house, dragging men and women out of their homes and throwing them into prison (Acts 8:3).

Now look closely at Acts 8:1: "On that day a great persecution broke out against the church in Jerusalem, and all except the apostles were scattered throughout Judea and Samaria."

Judea and Samaria sound familiar? Those are the regions the Lord told the disciples to go to in Acts 1:8. Because they stayed in Jerusalem, God gave them Acts 8:1—persecution.

We see God's overall purpose and plan unveiling in Acts 8:4: "Those who had been scattered preached the word wherever they went." God used persecution to get the good news outside of Jerusalem. Why? He has always meant for the gospel to reach the ends of the earth,[1] and the first Christians weren't taking it there. He is a God of global glory.

The key question then becomes: Why weren't the first Christians taking the gospel to the ends of the earth? I have asked many audiences that question, and they always come up with the same answers. They will say things like, "They didn't want to leave their homes," "They didn't want to leave their jobs," "They were worried about their children's education," "They didn't want to leave their extended family and friends," or "They didn't have the money to go."

All of these answers could well be correct, but they are given from a cat's perspective. To combat that, I try to encourage my audiences—and now you—to think through the ramifications of what this means.

What do the Scriptures show us? They show us that God had a *higher priority* than the first Christians' living in their own homes. He had a *higher priority* than their staying at their secure jobs and receiving their steady incomes. He had a *higher priority* than their families and friends and their children's education. He wanted to see his glory go out to the nations; therefore, he allowed his people to suffer.

This makes it sound like God loved the nations more than his people, but that is never the case. God loves all people (and peoples) equally.[2] How does his love shine equally?

Let's consider those who ran for their lives. It seems safe to assume that they weren't saying, "Praise the Lord! The Great Commission! Let's go reach the nations for Christ!" Did they have to trust God for food along the way? Yes. Did God provide? Yes. Did they have to trust God for places to stay? Yes. Did God provide? Yes. Did they have to trust God for their children's health and well-being and education? Yes. Did God provide? Yes. All of these things happened, and much more.

Now here is a simple question: What did this suffering do to their walk with God? I'm sure it caused it to grow tremendously. They saw God provide in ways they had never seen before. Their faith in God grew. Their love for God grew. Their dependence upon God grew. Throughout the entire process they became more like God.

When I speak to groups, I encourage believers to consider becoming missionaries—not only for the sake of the lost but for their own sake as well. Many Christians don't realize that most of their comfort and security, in reality, isn't in God. It's in their culture. In order for their security to come from God rather than from their culture, they need to leave the comforts of home.

In chapter 15 we mentioned four deaths: dying to ourselves, dying to our family and friends, dying to our national heritage and pride, and, finally, dying to humanity. Here we are referring to that third death—specifically by being willing to live outside of our own country. Believers need to experience dependence upon God in a whole new way as they are fashioned into his image through the challenge of cross-cultural living.

Open Doors International, an organization whose mission is to serve persecuted Christians worldwide, tells about a Chinese evangelist who wrote his wife the following words: "Without fire, how can gold become pure? Without chiseling, how can a rock become a statue? Without pressing, how can grapes become wine?"

Look at the following Scripture texts, and see how suffering makes us more like God:

- "Our fathers disciplined us for a little while as they thought best; but God disciplines us for our good, that we may share in his holiness."—Hebrews 12:10
- "We do not want you to be uninformed, brothers and sisters, about the troubles we experienced in the province of Asia. We were under great pressure, far beyond our ability to endure, so that we despaired of life itself. Indeed, we felt we had received the sentence of death. But this happened that we might not rely on ourselves but on God, who raises the dead."—2 Corinthians 1:8–9
- "And we boast in the hope of the glory of God. Not only so, but we also glory in our sufferings, because we know that suffering produces perseverance; perseverance, character; and character, hope."—Romans 5:2–4
- "But whatever were gains to me I now consider loss for the sake of Christ. What is more, I consider everything a loss because of the surpassing worth of knowing Christ Jesus my Lord, for whose sake I have lost all things. I consider them garbage, that I may gain Christ."—Philippians 3:7–8

All of these verses speak of becoming a mature believer. This is what discipleship is all about and what the church should be promoting. Believers who try to avoid suffering are locking themselves into an immature Christian life. As the great writer and theologian François Fénelon remarked, "The more we fear to suffer, the more we need to do so."

Not only will suffering draw us closer to God and make us more like Christ, but it will also intensify our eternal joy. Notice what Paul says in 2 Corinthians 4:17–18: "For this light momentary affliction is preparing for us an eternal weight of glory beyond all comparison, as we look not to the things that are seen but to the things that are unseen. For the things that are seen are transient, but the things that are unseen are eternal" (ESV).

What do you think the apostle means when he says that "affliction is preparing for us an eternal weight of glory"? The Greek word translated "preparing" is *katergazomai*, which literally means "to work fully" and by implication can mean "to perform, accomplish, achieve, work out, produce, etc." In other words, the suffering ("light momentary affliction") is "preparing" or "working out" or "achieving" a glory and joy for us beyond all comparison. There is a connection between suffering and the glory experienced in heaven.

If we take Paul's words in earnest, it seems that although we will all experience God's glory and joy, we will experience it in different degrees. We will all be full of joy, but we will experience it at different levels. Some will have a capacity for greater joy. That capacity was "prepared" or "achieved" through the suffering they endured.

Could these greater levels of joy be what Paul was referring to when he wrote of a "third heaven" (2 Corinthians 12:2)? Is this why he repeatedly spoke of "heavenly realms" or "heavenly places" (Ephesians 1:3, 20; 2:6; 3:10)? Is this why the writer of Hebrews mentioned Jesus passing through the heavens and being exalted above them (Hebrews 4:14; 7:26)?

Perhaps it is because varying degrees of joy can be experienced in heaven that Jesus could say, "Blessed are you when people insult you, persecute you and falsely say all kinds of evil against you because of me. Rejoice and be glad, because great is your reward in heaven" (Matthew 5:11–12).

Why rejoice? Because of the association between suffering and reward. What is the reward? Glory! What happens when we experience God's glory? We get joy! Hence the association can easily be made between suffering and joy. The more we suffer, the greater joy we experience eternally.

If this were not true, we would all experience the same amount of joy in heaven. In that case, why would our Lord tell us to rejoice in our sufferings? Why rejoice if we are all going to get the same amount of joy in heaven, no matter what? There is a link between suffering and greater eternal joy.

Think about it. If temporary suffering yields greater eternal joy, you can bet we would want to rejoice in it. As dog Christians who focus on the other side of the cross, we don't seek suffering, but we certainly don't shy away from it either. If we go through the suffering God has for us, it only creates a far greater and more everlasting joy than we will ever experience here on this earth.

This chapter has mainly addressed what suffering does for us personally. Now let's consider how our suffering can make an amazing impact on other people—for God's glory.

CHAPTER 20

How Your Suffering Affects Others

Primary writer: Bob

When you begin to focus on the other side of the cross, everything can change. Your focus is primarily on God's glory, and that spotlight breathes a new dimension on suffering. Open Doors International shares about a man named Mikhail Khorev, who wrote these words in prison: "Lord, if my bonds glorify you more than my freedom, why should I want freedom?"

How does a believer's suffering relate to God's glory?

In Matthew 13:44 we read a simple analogy that Jesus made about finding a treasure. A man finds a treasure, and then in his joy goes and sells all he has to buy that treasure. Whether you read the parable (like I do) as though God is finding us, or as though we are finding God, one aspect of what it has to say is the same: *Whatever you gladly give up shows the value of the treasure.* If you sell only a little, what you have here on earth is more valuable than the treasure itself; therefore, the treasure is not that valuable. If you sell a lot, the treasure must really be valuable. If you sell everything, the treasure must be infinitely valuable in your eyes.

For years, my sons loved going to basketball camp. When they were younger, my wife and I paid for the camp. But when they got older, we told them they had to pay for it themselves. At that point, going to basketball camp took on a different value. It wasn't worth the sacrifice of paying the tab. It wasn't really that valuable to them.

In his book *Let the Nations Be Glad!* John Piper says, "Loss and suffering, joyfully accepted for the kingdom of God, show the supremacy of God's worth more clearly in the world than all worship and prayer."[1]

How can suffering show God's worth more clearly than worship? Think about what would happen at a typical church in America on a hot, sweltering Sunday morning if the air conditioning stopped working. People would gripe and complain, and many would eventually leave. Why? They are willing to worship God in comfort, but when it comes to worshiping him in extreme conditions—well, quite honestly, he is not worth that much.

As Jesus' parable shows us, Christianity is about finding a treasure. We need to sell everything, giving up all our ease and comfort, if we want to find Christ. One of the greatest ways we can give up everything, thus showing the immeasurable worth of our God, is to suffer gladly for him.

It is for this very reason that people have left their loved ones and gone to the mission field. Revealing God's glory by reaching the nations was more valuable to them than their homes, jobs, families, and friends. They wanted to do Acts 1:8 without worrying about Acts 8:1. Their suffering says to God, "I'm going through this pain and isolation—having left my family, friends, job, and culture—as well as struggling to learn a new language, in order to show how very valuable you are by taking your glory to those who have never heard the good news!"

This is partially what Jesus was getting at when he said, "If anyone comes to me and does not hate father and mother, wife and children, brothers and sisters—yes, even their own life—such a person cannot be my disciple" (Luke 14:26). Jesus didn't mean that we literally have to "hate" our family members, but rather that our love for Jesus (showing him to be our greatest treasure and therefore extremely valuable) must be so great that our love for others looks like "hatred" in comparison. The problem isn't that we love our family too much; it's that we love God too little.

As others see us desiring God as our most valuable treasure, they will want what we have.

I remember when two Jehovah's Witnesses came to our door when we lived in Phoenix. As they began their rehearsed speech, I noticed that one of them had a pale, depressed look on her face. She seemed void of emotion. After they finished their opening speech, we talked for quite a while. And then I said to that woman, trying to do so in love, "Whatever it is you have, I really don't want anything to do with it. You look so depressed and worn out, I wouldn't want what you've found."

Compare this with what we see in the apostle Paul in his letter to the Philippians:

> I want you to know, brothers, that what has happened to me has really served to advance the gospel, so that it has become known throughout the whole imperial guard and to all the rest that my imprisonment is for Christ. And most of the brothers, having become confident in the Lord by my imprisonment, are much more bold to speak the word without fear.
>
> Philippians 1:12–14, ESV

Paul was anything but emotionless, even in his suffering. In fact, his joy was so full that the whole guard heard about it. We can only imagine the chatter spreading throughout the building. "Do you hear that guy singing? It's incredible. He has suffered so much, but he's still full of joy. Who is this 'Christ' he can't stop talking about?"

Paul's joyful suffering brought God additional glory by emboldening fellow believers to preach the gospel without fear, even though they too could be thrown in prison. They further displayed God's value to the world around them.

Like John Piper says, gladly suffering for the kingdom of God shows the supremacy of God's worth more clearly than worship and prayer.

This is the kind of idea Paul had in mind when he spoke of suffering for others in Colossians 1:24: "Now I rejoice in what I am suffering for you, and *I fill up in my flesh what is still lacking in regard to Christ's afflictions, for the sake of his body, which is the church*" (emphasis added).

What did Paul mean by "what is still lacking in regard to Christ's afflictions"? Didn't Jesus suffer enough for the sins of the entire world? Of course he did. Then what was Paul saying?

He was saying that there are those who are so rebellious in their will, so hardened in their hearts, that they need to see the suffering of Christ firsthand to be able to receive the good news. Yet because Jesus suffered at one fixed point in the history of humanity, they can't go back in time to see it. But Paul was saying, "If you missed it in Christ, then you can see it in us, his disciples, now. Our suffering will show you Christ's sufferings. It will be a secondhand experience, but it will show you what Jesus did for you and for the glory of the Father. Let it soften your hearts."

Michael Card tells a story that serves as a perfect example of this, a story about a Masai warrior named Joseph. When someone shared the gospel with Joseph, he accepted Jesus as his Lord and Savior. Joseph's life began to change, and he was filled with excitement and joy. He was eager to share the good news with the members of his village.

> Joseph began going from door-to-door, telling everyone he met about the Cross of Jesus and the salvation it offered, expecting to see their faces light up the way his had. To his amazement the villagers not only didn't care, they became violent. The men of the village seized him and held him to the ground while the women beat him

with strands of barbed wire. He was dragged from the village and left to die alone in the bush.

Joseph somehow managed to crawl to a waterhole, and there, after days of passing in and out of consciousness, found the strength to get up. He wondered about the hostile reception he had received from people he had known all his life. He decided he must have left something out or told the story of Jesus incorrectly. After rehearsing the message he had first heard, he decided to go back and share his faith once more.

Joseph limped into the circle of huts and began to proclaim Jesus. "He died for you, so that you might find forgiveness and come to know the living God," he pleaded. Again he was grabbed by the men of the village and held while the women beat him, reopening wounds that had just begun to heal. Once more they dragged him unconscious from the village and left him to die.

To have survived the first beating was truly remarkable. To live through the second was a miracle. Again, days later, Joseph awoke in the wilderness, bruised, scarred—and determined to go back.

He returned to the small village and this time, they attacked him before he had a chance to open his mouth. As they flogged him for the third and probably the last time, he again spoke to them of Jesus Christ, the Lord. Before he passed out, the last thing he saw was that the women who were beating him began to weep.

This time he awoke in his own bed. The ones who had so severely beaten him were now trying to save his life and nurse him back to health. The entire village had come to Christ.[2]

This is the kind of suffering that will bring people to Christ when preaching just won't do it. Some people's hearts will only soften at this point. They want to see how much you value the treasure. This is when we are "filling up what is still lacking in regard to Christ's afflictions."

Suffering gladly for the kingdom of God is the most powerful way to display God's glory. Believers who embrace the other side of the cross know this, and are therefore willing to suffer if called to do so.

"Lord, if my bonds glorify you more than my freedom, why should I want freedom?"

CHAPTER 21

Two Types of Suffering

Primary writer: Bob

Randy Cresswell joined the ranks of Frontiers during the very beginning of my ministry with that organization. Randy wanted to work where no one else was working, so he targeted what was then one of the toughest countries in the world: Mauritania.

Over the years of fulfilling the dream he believed God gave him, Randy got deathly sick multiple times. One time he almost drowned in a raging river while trying to rescue some military officers. On another occasion an explosive device blew up right in front of him, resulting in second-degree burns on 70 percent of his body. At times he was without food, water, or other basic necessities.

Randy has suffered to reveal the glory of his heavenly Father.

Carl Medearis is another missionary friend of mine who joined the ranks of Frontiers in the early days. Carl and his wife, who had the same type of entrepreneurial spirit as Randy, ended up seeking to reveal their Father's glory among a Muslim terrorist group.

Over the years, they too suffered. Their greatest challenge came one day when Carl was traveling with some other Christians in Iraq. A black Mercedes pulled up alongside them, and they suddenly found themselves driving down the road with machine guns pointed at their car. The signal was clear: pull over.

After complying and stopping on the side of the road, Carl and his friends were taken over a hill where no one could see them. Assuming they were being robbed, Carl thought through how much money he had on him. After being forced to his knees, however, it became clear that this was no robbery. Carl and his friends were going to be killed. Guns were pointed directly at their temples. Carl's life flashed before his eyes, and he prayed a simple prayer asking the Lord to take care of his wife and children.

Amazingly, by God's grace Carl survived after a series of miraculous circumstances. By God's grace, the hijackers didn't shoot Carl and his friends. Instead, they just left them by the side of the road.

Carl too has suffered to reveal the glory of his heavenly Father.

Keith Wheeler is another friend who has suffered to reveal his Father's glory among the nations.[1] Keith's ministry is carrying a twelve-foot wooden cross around the world and boldly proclaiming Christ's love for all people.

I met Keith recently while speaking at a missions conference at Columbia International University. Keith's role was to be the storyteller during the evening sessions. To encourage the students, he told stories about great victories while carrying the cross around the globe. Yet he balanced those stories with stories of great suffering. Keith has been arrested many times, and even thrown in jail. He has been beaten and left for dead.

One time when Keith was in Latin America, some people became so infuriated with him that a large number of men with machine guns came up to him and pointed the barrels at his face. As Keith stood next to his cross, they said to him (in Spanish), "We are going to count to three and then kill you."

Keith calmly began to explain how God loves them.

"Uno!" they said.

"God loves you. He died on the cross for you."

"Dos!" Click—their guns were now ready to fire.

"Jesus wants to set you free. You are so loved by God."

"Tre . . ."

And then, as Keith told the students, "I'm not sure what happened after that. All I can remember is that they were about twenty yards away and were putting their hands over their faces, saying, 'The light! It's so bright. I can't see!'"

Keith too has suffered to reveal his Father's glory to the nations.

Randy, Carl, and Keith all know that suffering to reveal the Father's glory is a normative part of the Christian life. It is the kind of life Jesus lived. It is the kind of life Paul lived. It is normal. When you live for the other side of the cross, suffering is part of the "package" of being a believer.

Most cat Christians would agree with this—in the missionary context. But they still have a problem with suffering when it's not related to missions. What happens when you're not on the mission field, when you're simply living a normal everyday life, and you suffer? Is that still God's will for you?

Is having your coworker lie about you to get ahead in the company the type of suffering God wants you to go through? Is being abused as a child the type of suffering God is referring to? Is being raped when you were baby-sitting at someone else's house the type of suffering God wills?

There seem to be two types of suffering. One type happens when you're strategically seeking to take the gospel to those who haven't heard it. The other type happens when you're not at all seeking to be strategic for God's glory. You're just living life, and yet something happens that causes you to suffer. Are both types of suffering equal in God's eyes? Does God appoint both types, or just allow them?

What about the suffering that occurs when the one who causes you to suffer has no idea you are a Christian? What if they hurt you solely out of their own free will? Maybe you were cheated in the business world. Perhaps a drunk driver hit your car head-on, leaving you paralyzed. Perhaps a stray bullet from a gang war took one of your children home to be with the Lord. In these cases, it didn't matter whether or not you were a believer. What about this type of suffering? Does God will this? Does God want this?

Let's look at the example of Joseph in the Bible. Joseph suffered greatly at the hands of his brothers. Because he spoke of his grandiose dreams, his brothers seriously thought about killing him. Not really wanting his blood on their hands, however, they sold him instead as a slave to some traders who happened to be passing by. Joseph wasn't treated this way because of his faith, but because he grew up in a very dysfunctional family.

As a slave, Joseph suffered tremendously. He had nothing to call his own, not even the clothes on his back. He couldn't come or go as he wished. He could eat only what was given to him. He had no freedom. In a very real sense, his life was not his own; he was owned by someone else.

Later, after serving his master faithfully and causing great blessing to come to his household, Joseph was thrown into prison because he was falsely accused of attacking his master's wife. Joseph spent years in that prison, suffering physically and emotionally.

You know the rest of the story. Following years in prison and some miraculous circumstances, Joseph became Egypt's second-in-command, accountable only to Pharaoh himself. He reunited his family (after a tremendously emotional ordeal), made peace with his brothers, and basically lived happily ever after.

After their father's death, however, Joseph's brothers feared his retribution. So they invented a story, evidently, saying, "Dad told us on his deathbed to ask you to forgive us for treating you so badly." Joseph responded to his brothers with these words: "Do not fear, for am I in the place of God? As for you, *you meant evil against me, but God meant it for good*, to bring it about that many people should be kept alive, as they are today" (Genesis 50:19–20, ESV, emphasis added).

Note that the word Joseph used for his brothers' actions was "evil." It is the same Hebrew word, *ra*, that is translated "evil" when referencing the Tree of Knowledge of Good and Evil in the garden of Eden in Genesis 2:9. The evil Joseph was speaking about was a culmination of events that began with his own arrogance (he wasn't trying to make God look good) and his brothers' free will.

Joseph said, "You meant evil against me, but God meant it for good." All evil that comes to us *is meant for our good*. That's why the Lord could proclaim in Jeremiah 32:40, "I will make an everlasting covenant with them: I will never stop doing good to them." *Whatever comes our way, whether blessings or evil, is meant for our good.*

It was because of this evil that the Lord was able to put Joseph into a position of great power and influence. *God is sovereign over all evil that occurs.* That key lesson is also found in the Book of Job, which teaches us that there is no differentiation between God allowing evil and willing evil. The two are the same to God. Whether he does it himself or uses Satan, he is still sovereign.

Interestingly, God's Word goes one step further. The Scriptures point to the idea that God not only allows evil but also ordains evil—even devises it. Let's look at two key passages.

In Isaiah 45:7 (emphasis added), the Lord says:

> I form the light and create darkness,
> I bring prosperity and *create disaster* [Hebrew *ra*];
> I, the LORD, do all these things.

God creates evil? That's what the text says. God is behind it all. He himself doesn't do evil, but he can use natural physical laws or the free will of others to send it to us.

In Micah 2:3 (emphasis added), we read:

> Therefore, the LORD says:
> "I am *planning disaster* [Hebrew *ra*[2]] against this people,
> from which you cannot save yourselves.
> You will no longer walk proudly,
> for it will be a time of calamity [*ra*]."

God allows and appoints—even devises—suffering in our lives. He allows the kind of suffering that occurs when we are taking his glorious message to our neighbors and to the nations, and he allows the kind of suffering that occurs when we are minding our business and bad things just happen to us. Both are from God.

As a believer, you are destined to suffer. You may not experience the extreme physical suffering that other Christians have endured (or are enduring), but you will suffer. Sleepless nights, broken windows, flat tires, 401(k)s that turn into 201(k)s, the pain of divorce or rape: such may be a part of the suffering God has—in his great love—for you.

No wonder Peter emphasized that believers shouldn't be surprised when trials come their way (1 Peter 1:6–7, 4:12–19). In fact, "those who suffer according to God's will should commit themselves to their faithful Creator and continue to do good" (1 Peter 4:19). Paul adds that we shouldn't be unsettled by our trials: "For you know quite well that we are destined for them" (1 Thessalonians 3:3).

But the bigger question is "Why?" Why would God allow suffering in the lives of those he loves? Why would he allow suffering in our lives even when we have been adopted as his children? How does that reflect his love for us?

CHAPTER 22

Ten Reasons Why God Allows Suffering

Primary writer: Kevin

God does everything in your life for one overarching purpose: to draw you closer to him so that you can see and delight in his glory—and therefore love him and serve him throughout all eternity. This objective includes God allowing evil into your life that results in suffering. If you understand the sovereignty of God, you know that *God could send Satan to the bottomless pit today and cease the church's suffering*. He doesn't choose to do that, however. He allows us to experience evil for a reason; the ensuing suffering is a tool that God uses in many ways.

Remember, Jeremiah 32:40 is *always* true. There the Lord said this about his people: "I will make an everlasting covenant with them: I will never stop doing good to them." God will never stop doing good to you. No matter what your circumstances, God can use even evil to reveal his glory and bring about good in your life. Like Paul stated in Romans 8:38–39: "I am convinced that neither death nor life, neither angels nor demons, neither the present nor the future, nor any powers, neither height nor depth, nor anything else in all creation, will be able to separate us from the love of God that is in Christ Jesus our Lord."

Let's go over some of the purposes of suffering. We have already touched on many of these in previous chapters, but we will review here and add more. This list isn't exhaustive, but it does give you a good idea of what God might be doing when he appoints suffering in your life.

#1: To Bring Judgment

One reason God may use evil is to bring judgment. In today's politically correct world we don't like to talk about judgment. It sounds cruel and hard. But mark it down: God still judges today, just as he judged Sodom and Gomorrah in the Old Testament and Ananias and Sapphira in the New Testament.

There are times when our sin reaches a point where God says, "That's it. Your sin is too great. It's time for judgment."[1] Bob and I believe a modern-day example of this is Saddam Hussein. God said, "Enough is enough," and raised up a foreign power to bring about a final judgment on this man.

"Jesus Christ is the same yesterday and today and forever" (Hebrews 13:8). God judged in the past. He still judges now.

#2: To Bring Us to Repentance

Many times God will allow suffering in order to bring about repentance in our lives. We can see this fact clearly in the Book of Jeremiah. In Jeremiah 32:42, we read, "This is what the LORD says: As I have brought all this great calamity on this people, so I will give them all the prosperity I have promised them."

At first glance this sounds completely contradictory. "I have brought you calamity, but I promise I'll bring you prosperity." We want to cry out, "Come on, God! Which one is it? How can it be both?"

To understand this verse you have to look at in its context. Jeremiah was a prophet during a very difficult time. While the Babylonian army was besieging Jerusalem (Jeremiah 32:2), God spoke to Jeremiah about all the evil the Israelites were doing (vv.

30–35). The Lord reiterated the theme we see repeatedly in Jeremiah's ministry: Judah would be handed over to the king of Babylon, and the people would be taken into exile. But then God immediately began to speak about bringing them back home and causing them to fear him for their own good (vv. 36–41).

Why would the Lord bring the Israelites back? Because after being sent into exile, the people would realize their sins and repent. After repenting, they would move out of God's wrath and into his grace; and God would return to all of the good that he wanted to do to his people by bringing them back to the Promised Land and blessing them. How do we know they repented? By the phrase "then you will know that I am the LORD." You see it used all throughout the Bible (e.g., Exodus 6:7; 1 Kings 20:13; Isaiah 49:23), including repeatedly in Ezekiel, who prophesied during the time of Judah's dispersion.

What was the purpose of the evil that Nebuchadnezzar, the king of Babylon, brought to God's people? To get them to repent. This is why Daniel, Shadrach, Meshach, and Abednego had such a strong witness in the midst of foreign captivity.

Is God still doing this today? Yes! I know firsthand, for example, that the Lord frequently uses divorce to bring the people involved to himself. As they suffer through a divorce, many individuals wake up spiritually, repent, and walk with God in a fresh new way. Although God hates divorce (Malachi 2:16), he allows it and uses it for his glory.

God uses evil to bring us to repentance.

#3: To Prune Us and Build Character in Us

God is very clear that he desires us to radiate his glory to those around us—from our neighbors to the nations. And he wants us to continue radiating his glory throughout eternity. Here on earth, however, there is a lot of garbage in our lives that keeps that from happening; and God wants to get rid of those barriers. As Proverbs

25:4 says: "Remove the dross from the silver, and a silversmith can produce a vessel."

When the defects in our lives are removed, we become a vessel God can use for his glory. The process of chipping away at the garbage ("dross") in our lives and becoming more like Christ starts now, here on this earth. God will do whatever it takes to make us more like his Son.

In chapter 11 we talked about becoming more like Christ, being transformed "from one degree of glory to another" (2 Corinthians 3:18, ESV). That transformational process of building character into our lives often requires suffering.

This was not a foreign concept to Jesus. Look at what the writer of Hebrews tells us about our Lord: "In bringing many sons and daughters to glory, it was fitting that God, for whom and through whom everything exists, should make the pioneer of their salvation perfect through what he suffered" (Hebrews 2:10).

Jesus himself suffered, and the Scriptures tell us that through his suffering he was made perfect. This is our goal as well. Jesus calls us to be perfect, like our heavenly Father (Matthew 5:48). That means we will have to suffer. That is why Peter wrote: "Therefore, since Christ suffered in his body, arm yourselves also with the same attitude, because whoever suffers in the body is done with sin" (1 Peter 4:1).

When we are "done with sin," we radiate Christ's glory better and are more like him. Therefore, if we are reaching that goal, we should be excited. That is why Paul could say, "We rejoice in our sufferings, knowing that suffering produces endurance, and endurance produces character, and character produces hope" (Romans 5:3–4, ESV).

The suffering we experience produces endurance, character, and hope.

#4: To Expand Our Joy in Heaven

We looked at this reason for why God allows suffering in chapter 19, "The Personal Benefits of Suffering," so I will keep this section short. Suffering is producing for us a joy that goes beyond all comparison. The more we suffer, the greater our joy will be in heaven.

Although we will all be joyful, we will experience different degrees of joy. Psalm 16:11 tells us that in God's presence we will be full of joy. Imagine three balloons of different sizes: a five-inch balloon, a ten-inch balloon, and a fifteen-inch balloon. If you blow up the three balloons, they will all be "full"—though they are different sizes. This helps illustrate how we will all be full of joy in heaven, though we will have different capacities. Those with fewer joys (smaller balloons) will be just as content as those with greater joys (bigger balloons). There will be no jealousy. It will be God who satisfies us, and we will be content—rejoicing with all who are celebrating God.

#5: To Become More Dependent upon God

The Scriptures are very clear that one of the reasons God allows suffering and hardship into our lives is to get us to become more dependent upon him. The more we are dependent upon God, the more glory he receives and the more his power can flow through us.

Paul wrote about this in 2 Corinthians 1:8–9: "We do not want you to be uninformed, brothers and sisters, about the troubles we experienced in the province of Asia. We were under great pressure, far beyond our ability to endure, so that we despaired of life itself. Indeed, we felt we had received the sentence of death. But this happened that we might not rely on ourselves but on God, who raises the dead."

When we rely on ourselves, we can do nothing of eternal significance. I used to wonder why Jesus said, "Apart from me you can do nothing" (John 15:5). Is this really true? Think about what humanity has done without apparent guidance from God. We have put men on the moon. We have created computers that can sort through billions of bits of information in a fraction of a second. We can save premature babies.

What does Jesus mean that we can do "nothing"? He means *nothing of eternal significance, nothing that will last forever or bear eternal fruit.* When we work in our own power and abilities—relying on ourselves—we can do nothing of that nature.

God allows struggles into our lives so that we will quit trusting in ourselves and begin depending upon him. When we depend upon God, we can accomplish far more of lasting significance, and we can give far more glory to him.

#6: To Encourage Others to Share Their Faith

As we saw in chapter 20, "How Your Suffering Affects Others," when the apostle Paul was imprisoned, he found that his circumstances encouraged others to share their faith (Philippians 1:12–14). Why?

Imagine the effect that Paul's imprisonment had on the believers who visited him. They were witnessing him undergo one of the worst things that could happen to a person. Yet the result of Paul's suffering for the gospel was a life full of joy. Philippians is even known as the New Testament's letter of joy—the word "joy," in its various forms, occurring some sixteen times.

This told them that the God Paul served was able to take care of him even during the worst of times. And therefore God would take care of them as well. It showed them that God must be extremely worthy for Paul to endure all of this suffering.

This is what your suffering, if endured for God's glory, will do to those around you. They will be encouraged and emboldened to share their faith. This is why Paul wrote: "Most of the brothers, having become confident in the Lord by my imprisonment, *are much more bold to speak the word without fear*" (Philippians 1:14, ESV, emphasis added).

#7: To Help Others Come to Know Christ

We also went over this point in chapter 20, so again I will be brief. There are some people who are so hard, so distant from allowing the Holy Spirit to touch their hearts, that they need to see someone willing to suffer for Christ so they can understand the true worth of our Lord. Suffering shows the value of Christ (see #10 below). Therefore others are much more willing to acknowledge, "I want what they've got."

By way of review, take a look again at what Paul had to say about this in Colossians 1:24: "Now I rejoice in what I am suffering for you, and I fill up in my flesh what is still lacking in regard to Christ's afflictions, for the sake of his body, which is the church."

#8: Suffering Allows Us to Comfort Others

Only a woman who has lost a child at birth can fully minister to another woman who has lost a child at birth. There are times when only those who have suffered as we have can really comfort us.

This is another reason why God sometimes allows us to suffer. He knows that future events are going to take place in which a person will need someone who has been through the same thing. Hence the Lord allows his children to suffer not only for their growth, but so they can minister to others as well.

Paul wrote about this beautifully in the first part of 2 Corinthians: "Praise be to the God and Father of our Lord Jesus Christ, the Father of compassion and the God of all comfort, who comforts us in all our troubles, so that we can comfort those in any trouble with the comfort we ourselves receive from God" (2 Corinthians 1:3–4).

#9: Suffering Prepares Us for Eternity

In the last chapter, we saw how Joseph endured great suffering because of his dysfunctional family. His suffering had nothing to do with his faith; it had nothing to do with his relationship with God. But Joseph's suffering was used by God to put him at Pharaoh's right hand as second-in-command of Egypt.

Many people might say, "I'd suffer too if God was going to make me the vice president of the United States!" Since we know that probably isn't going to happen, though, many of us would refuse to suffer. We have missed the point.

Our suffering prepares us for great things from God, but those great things may not necessarily happen during the eighty or so years we have here on earth. The preparation may be for great things in eternity.

Don't you know that you are going to judge angels (1 Corinthians 6:3)? Aren't you aware that we are coheirs with Christ (Romans 8:17)? Have you forgotten that when you are judged and found faithful you will be put in charge of many things (Matthew 25:21)? Surely you remember that no eye has seen and no ear has heard what God has prepared for those who love him (1 Corinthians 2:9). And has it slipped your mind that as an overcomer in this world you are going to sit with Christ on his throne throughout eternity (Revelation 3:21)?

Unless we live with an eternal mindset, we will never be able to see our suffering from the proper perspective. It is preparing us for eternal things that we can't even imagine. Don't give up hope.

#10: Suffering Magnifies the Value of Christ

This too we addressed in chapter 20, so we will review quickly here.

I was watching Glenn Beck one night as he interviewed a man who had walked out on his boss, knowing that he would be fired from his job if he did. He walked out because he received a phone call informing him that his dog had died and that his children were about to come home from school. He knew that some of his children would be devastated by the news, so he wanted to be with them. By leaving his high-paying job, he showed the value he put on his children.

This man helps us see that the more we suffer for something, the more we display the value of it. If we are breaking our backs to manage a large mortgage on a house, the worth of the house must be great in our eyes. If a young man drives eleven hours through sleet and snow just to see a young woman, she must be very special to him.

It is the same way with God. If we are willing to sacrifice and suffer in order to get God, we show that his value is very great in our eyes and in the eyes of others. On the other hand, if we aren't willing to sacrifice and suffer for God, he must not be very worthy.

Put in simple terms, suffering magnifies the value of God. It makes him look good, and that is what life is all about.

There are numerous reasons why God allows his children to suffer. Though this list of ten reasons isn't exhaustive, it can help people see why they are going through difficult times.

Cats try to avoid suffering at all costs. And if they are forced into trials, they don't go through them for God's glory; they try to get out of them as quick as they can for their own comfort. When dog Christians suffer, they know that God is doing something in them and through them to reveal his glory in wonderful and glorious ways. They realize that the only way to reveal this glory is to go *through* the difficult times, not around them.

CHAPTER 23

God's Greatest Glory: Why All Nations?

Primary writer: Bob

When Kevin and I were first developing this material, I called my friend Parke Slater to ask if I could speak at the church that meets in his home. I told him that I was working on a new teaching and needed to test it out. Parke and his church were delighted to accept the invitation to be the first group to hear it.

After the first lecture, I asked for feedback. They gave some great input. One of the things I learned from them was the need to communicate clearly what we are *not* saying. We are not saying that suffering is the highest goal in the Christian life. That is not true; living for God's glory is the highest goal. But living for God's glory will result in some level of suffering. And when it occurs, embrace it—don't run from it. If severe suffering doesn't come, that's fine too. But always be open to it for God's glory. Keeping God's glory as primary in everything we do is what our focus in life should be.

With that understood, a simple question can arise. How much glory do we want to bring God? Do we want to bring our Father some glory? Do we want to bring him a lot of glory? Or do we want to bring him maximum glory?[1]

Dog Christians desire to bring their Father maximum glory. And since you are still reading this book, I assume that is your goal and intent! So just how do we do that? How do we bring God the greatest glory he could ever have? That answer is found in two parts. The first is how we can individually bring God the greatest glory. The second is how we can corporately, as humanity, bring God the greatest glory. We will look at how we can individually bring God the greatest glory in the next chapter. In this chapter we will talk about how we can corporately bring God the greatest glory.

To understand how humanity can corporately bring God the greatest glory, we need to know a simple yet profound principle: God reveals more glory when he unifies that which is diverse.

Let me give you a personal example of this on a micro scale.

When Debby and I and our four kids first moved to Virginia, our family lived in harmony. We were all pretty much alike. We looked the same. We thought the same. We did most of the same things. There might have been little quarrels here or there, but no real fighting took place. God was being glorified by the harmony in our family.

When I speak on this topic at a church, I use PowerPoint to illustrate our family harmony by showing a slide in which the audience can hear three pianos all playing the same note at the same time. The sound isn't too impressive, but at least there is no disharmony.

Six months after we moved to Virginia, my mother moved from Pittsburgh to live with us. My father had died two years earlier, and this move was all part of the plan.

Although my wonderful mother was related to us through flesh and blood, there were some definite differences between us. My mom grew up during the Great Depression, so when she saw our children throw the leftover milk in their cereal bowls down the sink, she had a minor fit. "How could they waste all that milk?" She insisted that they drink it! We certainly talked with my mom about this one! And whenever our children left a room without turning off the lights, she said, "They're wasting so much money!"

Oh, how living together can bring out both the best and the worst in us. Because of all of this, my wife and I had to do some major "damage control" over the first few months and work through the issues with my mom. It caused all three of us to evaluate what was important and what was not. (We now unwrap our Christmas gifts carefully so that the paper can be reused!)

At this point in a seminar, I say that having my mom live with us was like no longer having three pianos but rather a piano, an oboe, and a flute—three generations—yet all still playing the same note. There was some definite diversity that was being unified. The PowerPoint audio that comes through the church's sound system is still rather unimpressive, but definitely better.

Three years after my mom moved in with us, she got a phone call from her old high school boyfriend. They hadn't talked to each other in sixty-three years! After finding her alive and well, he flew out to spend some time with her, and they both discovered that they were in love. A year later they were married, and then *they both lived with us!*

Cecil was an eighty-seven-year-old World War II veteran in failing health. We treated him like a king. Yet one night at the dinner table, Hunter, our youngest, asked, "Why doesn't Mr. Cecil ever have to do the dishes?" More lessons in unifying diversity in the household.

I communicate this by switching the PowerPoint slide from a piano, oboe, and flute all playing the same note to a piano, oboe, and flute playing a melody—though all three are playing the same notes at the same time. Very nice, and much better than all three instruments simply playing one note, but still not that impressive.

Many years later my daughter Elise, while she was in college, asked if her Arabic teacher from Tunisia could join us during their Christmas break. Her teacher would be in the United States for only a year, and Elise wanted her to experience what it was like to be in an American home at Christmastime. Because we know of God's high desire to bless internationals, we happily agreed.

Now my wife and I had four children, my mother and her husband, and an Arab woman in our home. No, we didn't serve our standard honey-glazed ham for Christmas dinner! But as we spent the holiday together, there was wonderful harmony as our diversities were unified in love. It was also a wonderful time to share about Christ with Elise's teacher.

At this point in a seminar, my audio files have a piano playing a melody and an oboe and a flute playing different harmonies. The sound is beginning to get rich and full—especially impressive compared to three pianos all playing the same note.

The following year, our niece became pregnant at the age of seventeen and had no place to live. So she moved in with us, and gave birth to her son when she was eighteen. Now we have four generations living with us, making for a very full house!

To expand the point, when diversity (different musical instruments—people from all nations) is unified (in harmony—through the blood of Jesus Christ), the richest sound (the glory of God) is revealed in greater ways.

This personal example was on the micro scale. Let's look at the same principle on a macro scale. Let's take, for example, a husband and wife who are on the verge of divorce. You see disharmony, and God uses you to show this couple what God's Word has to say. And then God heals their marriage through the application of the Scriptures. These two people (who hated each other days earlier) now stand in awe of God's healing power, and those intimately involved in their lives give God glory as they see what his Spirit has done.

Now let's say the Lord takes an Israeli soldier and a Palestinian soldier who are fighting each other with bitter hatred, and he draws them into a personal relationship with Christ. They end up putting down their guns and coming together through the blood of Christ, setting aside centuries of bitterness and animosity as they worship God arm in arm. The world really looks in awe at what God has done. Adding that to the reconciled couple, God will get even greater glory!

Now let's say the Lord adds to that scenario two Hindus who come to know Christ: one from the highest caste and the other from the untouchable caste. They now come arm in arm (note: they are touching each other!), worshiping God along with the reconciled couple and the two soldiers—and God gets even greater glory. Why? More diversity was unified! The principle continues: when more diversity is unified in Christ, God reveals more of his glory.

Add to that growing group new believers from the Aceh people of Indonesia, the Tajik of Afghanistan, the Amhara of Ethiopia, the Masai of Kenya and Tanzania, and the Qiang of China. Every time you add more diversity, God reveals more glory.

So imagine what it will be like when there are believers from every tongue, tribe, nation, and language. When all diversity is unified together through the blood of Jesus Christ, God's greatest glory will be revealed from humanity as we know it! How rich it will be! Instead of three instruments playing a song, a full orchestra will fill the air with the unity of diverse instruments all playing together in harmony.

I constantly challenge my audiences that this is the driving motivation for world evangelization. This is why God said he wanted people from *every* tongue, tribe, people, and nation. If even one nation were left out, God's glory wouldn't be revealed to the greatest degree.

I fully believe that this represents the heart of God revealed in his Word. God intended to create diversity so he could bring it back together in harmony, which in turn reveals his greatest glory.

Do we find any biblical evidence for this? Yes! We see it hinted at in Genesis 1:28 (the very first command to all of humankind through Adam and Eve) and Genesis 9:1 (the very first command to the second start of humankind through Noah and his family). In each case, God said, "Be fruitful and multiply and fill the earth" (ESV).

How does this hint at this principle? Well, what happens naturally to a language over centuries of time as people "fill the earth"?

The answer is simple: the language breaks down. First, accents are formed; then new words are created; and eventually, after many years have passed, an entirely new language is birthed. What is the result? Diversity.

Why did God want diversity? He wanted to unify it in his Son to reveal his greatest glory.

Yet we read in Genesis 11:1 that "the whole world had one language and a common speech." The people didn't want to "fill the earth." They said, "Come, let us build ourselves a city, with a tower that reaches to the heavens, so that we may make a name for ourselves; *otherwise we will be scattered over the face of the whole earth*" (Genesis 11:4, emphasis added).

In part because humankind didn't want to diversify, God did in one moment what would have normally taken centuries to do. He took their one language and broke it down into many different languages, creating instant diversity. The stage was now set for God to bring humanity back together in harmony through the blood of his Son, revealing his greatest glory.

Immediately after the nations were created in Genesis 11, God made a commitment to reach out to them. In the very next chapter he initiated a covenant with Abraham that consisted of two basic parts. In essence, God said to Abraham, "First, I want to bless you. Second, I want you to be a blessing to all the nations on the face of the earth—every one of them" (see Genesis 12:2–3).

This is where the Great Commission first begins! Like a set of railroad tracks (one rail is God's desire to bless us and the other rail is God's desire for us to be a blessing), it runs throughout the entire Bible, allowing us to read it as one book with one introduction, one story, and one conclusion. These two rails point to the greatest purpose: God's desire to reveal his greatest glory![2]

When Jesus, after his resurrection, reissued the Great Commission, he again emphasized "all nations" (Matthew 28:19)—every one of them. Why? Because if just one were missing, his greatest glory would not be revealed.

The beauty is that God's greatest glory is revealed at the end of it all. In Revelation 5:9, the angels before God's throne in heaven sing this "new song" to Christ the Lamb:

> You are worthy to take the scroll
> and to open its seals,
> because you were slain,
> and with your blood you purchased for God
> persons from every tribe and language and people and nation.

Note that this verse doesn't say "persons from *just about every* tribe and language and people and nation." It says "persons from *every* tribe and language and people and nation." The "all-ness" factor is complete.

In other words, what God set out to do (create diversity and bring it back together in harmony), he pulls off at the very end of time. This is the story of the Bible. It brings life together. It helps make sense of everything. *This is something worth living for. This is something worth suffering for. This is something worth dying for.*

Once you realize that the effort to reach all the nations is driven primarily by the motivation to glorify the Lord, the process becomes just as important as the end goal. You don't have to be an evangelical humanist who succeeds only when souls are won and churches are planted. You succeed as you seek to reveal God's glory every step along the way.

For missionaries, this means looking for, finding, and revealing the glory of God while raising support. That is just as glorious as winning souls. Trusting the Lord to learn a new language reveals the glory of God just as planting a church does. Believing God for new friendships in your target people group reveals the glory of God just as establishing elders does.

Everything should be done with the attitude of glorifying the Lord. This was Kevin's emphasis when he was the CEO of the non-profit organization. When you have that kind of attitude, *the process is just as valuable as the end result*. You will always come out winning, whether or not a church is established. Because you have been revealing God's glory all along, you will never have to come home from overseas with your tail between your legs.

Furthermore, you don't have to be a global worker to glorify God. Loving a child in your church's nursery brings glory to the Lord just as taking care of orphans in Mozambique does. Starting a new business in your hometown can reveal God's glory just as going overseas to plant churches does. Staying home and having a ministry in your "Jerusalem" doesn't make you a second-class Christian. We all can bring glory to the Lord!

Though you don't have to be a global worker, you do need to have a global mindset. This means that as you love the kids in your nursery you'll be praying that they somehow touch the nations as they get older. (Maybe you're holding a future missionary in your arms!) You'll be starting a new business in your hometown not so that you can get more money solely for yourself, but so that you can finance short-term and long-term workers. Don't forget that Acts 1:8 is a both/and—not an either/or nor a first/then!

Everything can be done, and should be done, to bring God glory. As Paul admonished in 1 Corinthians 10:31, "Whatever you do, do it all for the glory of God." This principle brings all of life together into one cohesive package: living to glorify the Lord. And we reach the nations as an act of worship primarily to reveal God's greatest glory. Learn this principle. Practice it. It can change your life!

CHAPTER 24

His Glory: Our Joy!

Primary writer: Kevin

We are talking about seeking to reveal God's greatest glory. In the last chapter we saw that this is done in a corporate sense when people from every nation worship God. Now let's look at this topic from a personal perspective.

As God seeks to reveal his greatest glory, a cat may be thinking, *OK, now I understand that it's about God revealing his greatest glory. But is there anything in there personally for us? God still loves us, right?*

Yes, cat, he does. And we've got great news for you!

To help the cat within us (no one is a perfect dog!), we need to understand the connection between God's love for us, God's glory, and our joy. The story of Jesus raising Lazarus from the dead, recorded in John 11, clearly shows us that connection. Notice how the story begins:

> Now a certain man was ill, Lazarus of Bethany, the village of Mary and her sister Martha. It was Mary who anointed the Lord with ointment and wiped his feet with her hair, whose brother Lazarus was ill. So the sisters sent to him, saying, "Lord, he whom you love is ill." But when Jesus heard it he said, "This illness does not lead to death. It is for the glory of God, so that the Son of God may be glorified through it."

> Now Jesus loved Martha and her sister and Lazarus. So, when he heard that Lazarus was ill, he stayed two days longer in the place where he was.
>
> John 11:1–6, ESV

John Piper helps us see the connection between love and glory in these first few verses.[1] Note how the apostle John talks about Mary having anointed Jesus' feet. Since John doesn't record that story until later (the next chapter, John 12), why does he mention it here? It seems that he wants to show the strong love between Mary and Jesus. John then continues to build on the love theme when the sisters send word to Jesus about Lazarus, "whom you love."

Verse 4 begins to shed light on glory. Jesus said that Lazarus was sick for one primary purpose. "It is for the glory of God, so that the Son of God may be glorified through it." Now we see a connection between glory and love. *Because Jesus loved this family, he wanted it to see God's glory.*

The key point of the text comes in verse 6. Many translations begin the verse with the word "so." The Greek word can also be translated "therefore." The thrust of the verse seems to be: "Hearing that Lazarus was ill, Jesus therefore chose to stay two days longer in the place where he was." What happened as a result of Jesus waiting two days? Lazarus died.

Make sure you get this straight. Because Jesus loved Lazarus, Mary, and Martha, he stayed where he was to let Lazarus die. Does that sound kind of weird to you? It should. Jesus loves a family, and therefore he lets one family member die? From today's "health and wealth" Christianity, we would expect that when Jesus heard that someone was sick, he would immediately go and heal him. That's how the text *should* read. But it doesn't. Why?

Lazarus's death was going to result in God being glorified. If you're having a hard time understanding this passage, let me give you a hint. It's a whole lot easier to understand if you place a higher priority on God's glory than on life itself. If God's glory has a higher priority, then this passage can be easily understood. We should be willing to die to let God's glory shine through us.

And for a dog Christian, letting someone you love die for God's glory is certainly acceptable. That is why parents who love the other side of the cross not only are open to their kids taking his glory overseas (even to the Muslim world), but also encourage them to do so—even if it means they might die. Death is just another means of revealing God's glory (see John 21:19). That is what Jesus was allowing to happen: Jesus let Lazarus die for the glory of God.

Now let's go to the part of the story in which Jesus raises Lazarus from the dead:

> Then Jesus, deeply moved again, came to the tomb. It was a cave, and a stone lay against it. Jesus said, "Take away the stone." Martha, the sister of the dead man, said to him, "Lord, by this time there will be an odor, for he has been dead four days." Jesus said to her, "Did I not tell you that if you believed you would see the glory of God?" So they took away the stone. And Jesus lifted up his eyes and said, "Father, I thank you that you have heard me. I knew that you always hear me, but I said this on account of the people standing around, that they may believe that you sent me." When he had said these things, he cried out with a loud voice, "Lazarus, come out." The man who had died came out, his hands and feet bound with linen strips, and his face wrapped with a cloth. Jesus said to them, "Unbind him, and let him go."
>
> John 11:38–44, ESV

Martha didn't believe that Jesus would raise her brother from the dead. She believed he could have healed his sickness, but she didn't believe he could raise him from the dead. She was basically saying,

"Lord, don't be ridiculous. There's a stench in there. You don't want to smell that."

Where did Jesus take Martha with her unbelief? Did he scold her? Did he rebuke her? No. He simply pointed her back to the glory of God, indirectly communicating, "The glory of God can do anything."

Jesus then raised Lazarus from the dead. God's glory was revealed in a way that it had never been revealed before, and Jesus was glorified because it was through him that God did this miracle.

Do you see what was happening? Jesus loved Martha, Mary, and Lazarus so much that he was willing to go to extreme measures to show them God's glory. When God loves someone, he wants them to see his glory; and he will do some extraordinary things to get them to see it.

Here is the key to satisfying the cat in all of us and understanding how God's glory relates directly to us as individuals.

Consider how much joy God wanted Martha and Mary to experience through this situation. Had Jesus healed Lazarus while he was sick, they surely would have been extremely thankful and happy. There would have been great joy. Their sick brother would be healthy. But consider how that joy would have compared to the joy they experienced in seeing the resurrection of Lazarus. I would submit to you that *their joy was far greater. The greater the degree of God's glory, the greater their joy.* This is one of the places where we see this principle: the more God's glory is experienced, the more our joy is realized.

This, we believe, is the reason Jesus allowed Lazarus to die. *Because he loved them,* he wanted Mary and Martha to experience *greater joy* as a result of seeing the glory of God revealed through Jesus raising Lazarus from the dead rather than healing his sickness.

The story of Lazarus being raised from the dead was about the glory of God being shown in power and authority, but it was also about *joy*. Experiencing God's glory in a greater way results in greater joy.

Now, considering this direct link between God's glory and our joy, I am going to connect two verses that together help us see why God is so excited about us coming to heaven.

Look at what Jesus said in John 17:24:

> Father, I want those you have given me to be with me where I am, and *to see my glory*, the glory you have given me because you loved me before the creation of the world. (emphasis added)

Why is Jesus so passionate about us seeing his glory? Is he egotistical? Is he moping in the heavens, wondering if anyone thinks he is glorious? No. For one thing, 1 Corinthians 13:5 tells us that love is not self-seeking. I would propose that the reason Jesus wants us to see his glory is because he wants our joy to be full.

Let's connect John 17:24 with Psalm 16:11:

> You make known to me the path of life;
> in your presence there *is fullness of joy;*
> *at your right hand are pleasures forevermore.*
> (ESV, emphasis added)

Why is there fullness of joy in God's presence? Because we see him in his glory. That's why he wants us to see him in his glory.

God knows that life has been a bummer for most people. Maybe your marriage didn't come out the way you dreamed it would. Maybe your kids gave you more grief than blessing. Perhaps work was a pain most of the time. Overall, you never really experienced a deep, abiding love in your heart. Jesus hurts for your pain, and he wants you to see his glory—because he loves you and wants you to be happy!

What will happen when we get to heaven? Isaiah 35:10 tells us, "Everlasting joy will crown their heads. Gladness and joy will overtake them."

Did you notice those last words? "Gladness and joy will *overtake them*." Why will it overtake us? Seeing his glory will be so wonderful, so unspeakable, and so awesome that we will be overcome with emotions of gladness and joy. What a day that will be!

Keeping in mind that the more God's glory is experienced the more our joy is realized, we now see how we can individually reveal God's greatest glory. How? By seeing and delighting in his glory above anyone or anything else.

Delighting in God's glory is one of the best ways we as individuals can reveal his glory and find great joy. And when this principle is applied to world evangelization, it all comes together. When every tongue, tribe, and nation is reached, God's greatest glory will be revealed. And when we see God's greatest glory revealed, we will have the greatest joy! Revealing his greatest glory results in our greatest joy! Therefore, we reach the nations not only for God's greatest glory but also for our greatest joy!

CHAPTER 25

The Missionary's Best-Kept Secret

Primary writer: Kevin

OK, it's time for us to spill the beans. This chapter might upset some missionaries, but we feel it's important for this secret to get out.

Being missions mobilizers, Bob and I have the unique opportunity to travel all over the United States and interact with many congregations and Christian organizations during their missions conferences or other missions-emphasis events. It's always interesting to listen to missionaries as they share what is happening on the frontlines of the kingdom as God's glory is advancing. It's even more interesting, though, to watch as the people in the pews digest this information. Oftentimes the members of the church come away recalling all of the apparent sacrifices and hardships our brothers and sisters on the field deal with: eating the strange food, living in harsh conditions, learning difficult languages, homeschooling their children, and, perhaps worst of all, enduring the horrendous potty conditions in some of those places!

Of course, the audiences also pick up that souls are being won and churches are being planted. Therefore they gladly make their "faith promise" missions pledge, thankful they have been left here in America to contribute to missions monetarily while they enjoy their "comfortable middle class life," as Scott Wesley Brown mentions in his song "Please Don't Send Me to Africa."

After the conference is over, the missionaries head back to the hardships of the field, and the typical American Christian family settles back into normal life. For most people, this normal life means worrying about their bills, their career goals, and their children's education.

In the midst of their worrying, they are entrenched in their daily activities: the parents hustle to work, dropping the kids off at school along the way. At the appointed time, they text each other to figure out who picks up each child after school, since one has to be at a piano lesson and another at soccer practice.

Family time commences promptly at 7:30 p.m., after both parents and kids come home. Family time consists of heating up a frozen pizza for dinner and watching TV while the kids check their Facebook and Mom and Dad return e-mails from the latter part of the workday. Then it's off to bed in order to get up and do it all over again. Only five more months until family vacation!

Bob and I are fairly sure that you can relate to most of this "normal life." We're not so sure you have seen things from the other vantage point, however. The missionaries have hidden a dirty little secret. We have traveled all over the world and have been able to observe dozens of different missionaries going about their daily lives. What we are about to share is in no way intended to downplay the sacrifices that our brothers and sisters make on the field. Those sacrifices and hardships are numerous, including living in environments where their lives and their children's lives are in danger—very real danger.

Nevertheless, along with that comes something that makes all the sacrifices seem paltry: joy! It seems that there is something about living life totally sold out for Jesus and passionately laboring to see his glory advance that taps into joy in a way that few other things in the Christian life can. You see, the unity we discussed in the last chapter is applied here: *God's greatest glory and our greatest joy go hand in hand.*

Not long after finishing college, I had the honor of taking my father with me on a short-term mission trip. We had a wonderful time serving God together by building churches, schools, and a radio tower in remote parts of South America. We ended up taking a few trips like this together after Dad retired. We enjoyed the whole adventure, but our favorite time of the day was when the work was done and the team of eight or nine men gathered for the evening meal. We were serving a missionary who had labored in that area for more than thirty years; John was just a couple of years younger than my retired father.

Each night around the dinner table John recounted stories of things that had happened throughout his long career. Hearing his adventures of trekking through the mountains and building huts for his family were eye-opening enough, but we also learned of his work among the native Indians, his close encounters with death, and the interaction he had with leftist guerrilla forces. Listening to John was like listening to someone who had lived a real-life version of an action adventure movie, or like being engrossed in a novel that you can't put down.

It wasn't just the stories that kept us spellbound; it was the way in which John shared those stories. They weren't just an account of his life; they *were* his life. He shared each story with a passion and joy that screamed, "I live to make God famous, and I love it!" This joy was evident in his eyes, his smile, his body language, and his enthusiasm.

Many years later, I flew to a remote part of Asia as part of a team. This was my first trip to Asia. Our goal was to observe the work taking place in multiple cities and report back to the supporting churches that had sent out the workers. The missionary teams were endeavoring to plant churches among a totally unreached people group spread across many miles.

Our first stop took us to one of the largest cities in Asia. I was immediately struck with the differences of the culture, the smells in the air, and the feel of the city. It occurred to me that I was "not in Kansas anymore"—or in my case, not in *Ar*kansas.

I remember chatting with a member of the church-planting project, a young man in his late twenties, who had come to greet us in this city. As the realization hit me that Mike was also far removed from his home, I wondered how he liked living here. He was making tremendous sacrifices by being away from home, out of his culture, living on support, etc. So I inquired, "How do you like living here?"

Mike's answer was not what I expected. He looked at me with a gleam in his eye and a smile on his face and said, "Are you kidding? It's freakin' Asia! I love it!" This was hardly the "Woe is me—someone has to make the sacrifice" answer I thought I would hear. As I looked around, thinking how far removed I was from my Western culture, the air of adventure started to hit me. This young man was beginning to remind me of John, the older missionary in Latin America.

The next day my eyes were opened even further to the joy that God's global workers experience. We flew to a much more remote city, made up of Buddhists and Muslims, where another part of the team was based. This city was not only miles away from the large urban center, but also further away in terms of culture. The conditions contrasted sharply with that large urban center, which now, in my mind, had become a clean modern city.

As we got acclimated to this city, I had a chance to get to know my new friend Mike, the twenty-nine-year-old global worker, a bit better. I learned how much he truly loved living in one of the remotest parts of Asia, and how much he loved God and the people he was endeavoring to reach. He told me stories of trekking through the mountains, traveling on horseback, riding on public sleeper buses, sleeping in monasteries, and eating raw yak meat. Mike wasn't kidding when he told me he really loved the life he lived as a result of following God wholeheartedly. At the end of one of our conversations, he said, "I thank God every day for saving me from the middle-class American life."

The next leg of our trip was an eighteen-hour bus ride through the high mountains to the city that is the cultural home of the people group we were targeting. We used two buses and a Jeep Cherokee that was owned by our group and driven by a hired national driver. Each of the team members, host workers, and their families packed into the buses while our luggage was crammed into the Jeep, along with Mike, my new Asia-loving, God-glorifying friend.

The long journey was a once-in-a-lifetime experience: taking in the stunning mountains and observing the indigenous peoples with their beautiful children at our stops along the way. All the while, we were becoming more and more distanced from Western civilization. I recall one roadside stop for a restroom break. The term "restroom" is used here in its cultural context, as it was nothing like any of us from the good ole USA would envision. I had already experienced my first "squatty potty," but this took even that term to a whole new level.

I walked up onto the makeshift platform—a plywood floor with a hole cut in it. Below the hole was a pile of waste, sitting outdoors underneath the platform. Peering through the hole, I could see pigs foraging around in the waste. Ugh! But when ya gotta go, ya gotta go! Yes, we were *far* from Kansas, and each new day showed us how vast the difference could be.

At about three in the morning, two to three hours from our destination, a light rain was falling in a misty fog. I was trying to get some sleep. I had dozed a bit, but was awakened when both buses stopped moving. Mike was on the side of the road, waving his flashlight. While going around a bend, the Jeep that was carrying our luggage had slid on the wet mountain road and tumbled down the side of the hill about two hundred feet, finally coming to rest upside down. Mike was able to extract himself from the wreckage and scurry back up the hillside just in time to flag down the buses, but the driver was still stuck in the Jeep.

We rescued the driver and took both him and Mike to the nearest hospital. Thankfully Mike only had minor injuries; and the driver, though his injuries were a bit more severe, recovered fully as well. Through this experience the driver responded to the gospel and joined the family of God!

After all the excitement caused by the accident died down, we toured the city and met local people as well as other global workers laboring there. We took in a festival in the city, toured monasteries, and met with some of the top religious leaders.

Our trip was capped off with a visit to a very small village a few hours from the target city in the mountains. We took a couple of Jeeps to the main village and then hiked the rest of the way to what our team called the "widows' village." Our workers' projects there included relief and development work for the widows in the village and making some microloans to help with the agriculture.

After the several-hour journey, we entered the village to encounter a small throng of villagers lining the road. They were dancing, singing, and playing the local music. It was a real-life image of the verse, "How beautiful on the mountains are the feet of those who bring good news" (Isaiah 52:7). I prayed that God would hasten the day when these people would sing and dance for him and his glory. After our initial greeting, they treated us to more dancing, singing, and horsemanship demonstrations.

Did I mention I love being a mobilizer?

After that exciting day, our group prepared to sleep in tents along the banks of one of the longest rivers in Asia. Before we went down for the night, a couple of the full-time workers, who had picked up that I enjoyed a few personal freedoms from time to time, invited me, as well as my senior pastor and worship pastor, down to the river. There we enjoyed cigars along with some really bad Asian beer. As we were smoking the cigars and drinking the beer, I experienced a fellowship with my brothers that I rarely experience back in the States. They were fully alive, and I was alive with them.

As I gazed at the river and the glistening stars overhead, I thought about the life these men and their families lead. They were glorifying God through endeavoring to plant a church among these people in this remote area of the world. It hit me that *they were privileged.* The words of the character William Wallace, from the movie *Braveheart*, echoed in my head: "Every man dies. Not every man really lives."

Missionaries really live! It's their best-kept secret, and it needs to be known.

CHAPTER 26

Why the Church?

Primary writer: Kevin

In addition to speaking in churches, Bob and I frequently teach sections of the Perspectives on the World Christian Movement course. This course, a ministry of the U.S. Center for World Missions, is held at churches and college campuses all over America. We recommend it to *every* Christian, regardless of what your role is in revealing God's glory to the nations.[1]

Whenever I speak to a Perspectives class, I always end by asking this question: "Why did God give the Great Commission to the church?" Now keep in mind that when I ask that question I have just taught for two hours on the importance of the glory of God and the Lord's desire to receive worship from people from every tongue, tribe, and nation. The answer I usually receive is that God gave the Great Commission to the church, ultimately, to bring about worship from every tongue, tribe, and nation. Although that is not incorrect, it is incomplete. It's true that worship from all peoples is part of the answer, but God could achieve that without the church—for example, by giving individuals dreams and visions.

For some seemingly insane reason, God gave the church this crazy task of revealing his glory to all nations (all ethnic groups) on the planet. Is God a masochist who wants us to suffer and sacrifice while trying to accomplish some seemingly impossible worldwide endeavor? Of course not.

In helping Perspectives students grasp God's purposes in giving the Great Commission to the church, I refer them to John Piper's book *Let the Nations Be Glad!*:

> Missions is not the ultimate goal of the church. Worship is. Missions exists because worship doesn't. . . . Worship, therefore, is the fuel and goal in missions. It's the goal of missions because in missions we simply aim to bring the nations into the white-hot enjoyment of God's glory. The goal of missions is the gladness of the peoples in the greatness of God. . . . But worship is also the fuel of missions. Passion for God in worship precedes the offer of God in preaching. You can't commend what you don't cherish. . . . Missions begins and ends in worship.[2]

The part of this quote that I highlight is the fact that worship is both the fuel and the goal of missions. Yes, we are trying to plant a church, and doing so will bring God glory. However, the act of the church embracing this humanly impossible task of reaching all nations is, in and of itself, an act of worship that God desires. Why?

Think about individuals who step out in faith to plant a church where none exists. What do they have to go through? First they have to trust God to raise support (typically a one- to two-year process). Then they go overseas to a culture totally foreign to them. There they have to find a place to live, learn a new language, get a job to stay in the country, develop friendships, and share their faith—trusting that God will open hearts to the good news. These huge steps of faith are acts of worship that reveal God's glory!

Now imagine yourself in God's place. If you are a jealous God (which we know from Exodus 20:5) and you are going to reach the nations for your glory, either you can do it yourself by writing in the clouds, or you can have a young family become so enamored with you and your glory that it is willing to step out in faith, raise support, go to a foreign country, suffer culture shock, struggle with how to educate its children, live in what can be very dangerous conditions, and endeavor to plant a church. Which method will bring you more glory? The latter! Those steps of faith made by his children bring God far more glory than if he did it by himself.

Not only do those steps bring God more glory, but they also bring more joy to those he uses. Joy was designed to follow great steps of faith. Why? Because when God comes through, you have touched something supernatural, and that births joy. Therefore, the young couple who is struggling to take God's glory globally has a joy waiting for them that they would not have experienced staying home in their comfort zone. Trusting in God and seeing him come through happen far more often outside your comfort zone than it does inside it. This is where the marriage takes place between God's greatest glory and your greatest joy.

Although most Christians living in their own culture don't know it, their comfort and security are found far more in their culture than they are in their God. They know the value of a dollar. They know how to greet each other. They can speak the language. They know how to get anywhere they want to go. They know how to find a place to live. They don't wrestle with culture shock. And they don't need to ask God for their daily bread—they just need to go to the nearest store.

Do believers who stay in their comfort zone have joy? Yes, but we would contend that in most cases it is shallow compared to the joy that believers in a culture not their own can experience.

When Christians leave their culture, they don't know the value of the strange coins in their pockets. They don't know how to speak the language. They don't know how to interact with the people around them. They aren't sure how to get from one place to the next, much less find a place to live. They don't even know where to go to buy bread. On top of all that, their lives, and the lives of their children, may be in much greater danger than at home.

What do they do? They cry out to God, "Help!" And when he does, something supernatural happens, and they get excited. This experience of God at work in their lives produces more joy. When this type of joy is evident, it naturally brings individuals and nations to the object of this effort and affection: to the One who gives that joy. Can this joy be discovered while staying in your own culture and living for the glory of God? Yes. But there is a far greater guarantee of finding it in a cross-cultural setting.

Their act of worship by putting their lives on the cross-cultural altar also brings God great glory. It demonstrates his worth by showing how much they (his children) value him and how much they want others to see his glory. The sacrifices they make radiate God's glory far more than praying and worshiping within a comfortable lifestyle.

Missions, joy, and glory are all beautifully connected. Like three strands in a cord, they weave together perfectly. God doesn't want our security to rest in our culture. He wants it to reside in him. He doesn't want our joy to be weak. He wants it to be full. He doesn't want some glory. He wants the greatest glory. *Therefore, he has given us—the church—the Great Commission for our sake. God loves us too much to allow us to settle for second best. He calls us to the other side of the cross, where there is glory for him resulting in true joy for us.*

Have we minimized the dangers and challenges that face those who take God's glory globally? We hope not—that was not our desire. Situations on the mission field don't always have a happy ending. For instance, things could have worked out differently for my missionary friend and the driver when the Jeep rolled off that mountain road.

I had to face the possibility of an unhappy ending myself just a year or so later when my wife, Kathleen, and our two kids, Kevin Jr. and Ashley, made that very same trip and went over that very same mountain road. I felt fear and angst within me when their bus didn't arrive within the eighteen hours it should have taken. I was at home in the States, communicating with people in Asia via phone and e-mail as I waited to be notified of their safe arrival.

Eighteen hours came and went, as did twenty hours, twenty-four hours, thirty hours, thirty-five hours. Each hour filled me with the realization that something bad could have happened. I had to acknowledge to God that he was in control, not me. After forty hours, I was very nervous when word finally came that they had arrived, delayed because the bus had broken down. It was a happy ending, but happy endings don't always come.

The truth is that the church of Jesus Christ is built on the blood of the martyrs—those who have died in the effort to see God's glory shine where it was not being revealed. Pick up *Foxe's Book of Martyrs*[3] or DC Talk's book *Jesus Freaks*,[4] and read some of the incredible stories. Or go to John Piper's website, DesiringGod.org, and read or listen to his message "Doing Missions When Dying Is Gain."[5] Or search for Piper's "Christians Must Suffer" message on YouTube.

You will be reminded that not every ending is happy, but you will also note that there are joyful endings. It seems that when believers are totally given to glorifying God, the Lord fills them with such joy and peace that they can agree with Paul's bold statement: "I consider everything a loss because of the surpassing worth of knowing Christ Jesus my Lord" (Philippians 3:8).

If dying really is gain, and if Jesus really is the treasure of our lives, it will show as we put aside the perceived benefits of the comfortable middle-class life and demonstrate that our careers are not our treasure, our hobbies are not our treasure, neither our churches, nor our ministries, nor even our children, nor our very lives are our treasure. Christ alone is our treasure! When we live that way, we fit a key into a supernatural lock and release glory for God and joy for us. There is glory and joy when we live for the other side of the cross. And the other side of the cross is sometimes best viewed from the mission field.

Although God gives us the Great Commission to a large degree for our sake, we can experience great pain in the midst of this task. Just ask the widows who have lost their husbands on the mission field. Ask the parents who have lost children serving on the field. There can be great pain. Life is not one big bowl of cherries.

Yet even in the pain there can be joy. Bob loves to share the story Floyd McClung tells about Corrie ten Boom. Floyd met Corrie when she was eighty-one years old. She told him that an angel informed her that her heavenly Father was going to give her ten more years to live. Five years later, Floyd met Corrie again, but this time she was in a hospital bed, suffering tremendous pain. Corrie told Floyd that the angel of the Lord alerted her that the pain and suffering she was going through was going to result in her death, and she was never going to get better.

Corrie said to the angel, "But I've got five more years to live."

The angel answered, "Yes, your heavenly Father knows that, and he's willing to take you home early."

Corrie asked, "What will bring my Father the most glory: coming home early or staying here for five more years?"

The angel answered, "Staying for five more years and suffering."

Corrie then replied, "I'll stay."

Corrie understood James 1:2: "Count it all joy, my brothers, when you meet trials of various kinds" (ESV). Why *joy*? Not because of what would come to Corrie—she got pain and severe suffering—but because she lived to radiate her Father's glory. And the joy of glorifying her Father (the reason for which she was created) outweighed the pain she was going to have to endure.

Corrie's pain, and the pain of those on the mission field, not only produces a joy the world will never understand, but it somehow molds and shapes believers to better reflect the glory of the Lord for his eternal purposes. Although joy and glory go hand in hand in missions, they don't hold the same importance. Dog Christians understand that glory is the highest priority. Everything else is secondary.

For the sake of glorifying his name, God may ask us to make tremendous sacrifices, just like his Son did. We should embrace this. At the same time, God has given us, the church, the Great Commission for our sake—so that we can embrace a joy that most people will never experience in their own culture.

Conclusion

Have you found the theology in this book to be rock solid? We hope you have. In the introduction to this book, we showed how certain theologies can be applied only at certain times.

Joseph glorified God greatly as a slave, a prisoner, and as second-in-command to Pharaoh. Christians who are focused only on the cat's side of the cross miss that foundational theme running through Joseph's entire life. It wasn't about becoming second-in-command; it was about glorifying God wherever he was.

Jesus glorified his Father in everything he did (John 17:4), even in his death. The Macedonian churches glorified God by giving out of their extreme poverty (2 Corinthians 8:2). Paul glorified God greatly by enduring beatings (without miraculous healings) and continuing to preach the good news (2 Corinthians 11:16–29).

Do you realize what this means? Do you realize what God has done for each of us? He has made it so that there is no situation, no circumstance, and no financial quandary you can find yourself in where you cannot live for the glory of God. No wonder Psalm 112:6 says, "Surely the righteous will never be shaken."

We have embraced and written about a rock-solid theology that can be lived out by the poorest people in Asia and Africa and by the wealthiest people in the Western world. It applies not only to an American who is externally blessed, but also to a Chinese pastor who has been in prison for twenty-two years. It can be lived out as a single person, as a child, as a student, or as a marketplace missionary. It should be the goal of marriage, parenting, and personal finances. It keeps us focused when we lose our job or get cancer.

We can have victory no matter what life throws at us. By living for God's glory, we are set free.

We encourage you, therefore, to live, focus, and meditate on the other side of the cross.

—Bob and Kevin

Notes

Introduction

1. Daniel R. Sanchez, *Church Planting Movements in North America* (Fort Worth: Church Starting Network, 2007), 18.
2. Reggie Joiner, Chuck Bomar, and Abbie Smith, *The Slow Fade: Why You Matter in the Story of Twentysomethings* (Colorado Springs: David C. Cook, 2010), 23.
3. "Do Americans Change Faiths?" Barna Group, August 16, 2010, http://www.barna.org/faith-spirituality/412-do-americans-change-faiths.
4. George Barna, *Revolution* (Carol Stream, IL: Tyndale, 2005), 49.
5. George Barna, *The Second Coming of the Church* (Nashville: Word, 1998), 13, 49, 54, 64–66.
6. David Barrett and Todd Johnson, *World Christian Trends* (Pasadena, CA: William Carey Library, 2001), 656.
7. "Abortion Facts," The Center for Bio-Ethical Reform website, http://www.abortionno.org/index.php/abortion_facts/.
8. "Go Figure," *Christianity Today*, December 2005, http://www.christianitytoday.com/ct/2005/december/7.22.html.
9. Patrick Johnstone, *The Church Is Bigger Than You Think* (Tain, Scotland: Christian Focus Publications, 1998), 181.

Chapter 1: Conflicting and Confusing Communication

1. That is, the Perspectives on the World Christian Movement course. For more information, visit www.perspectives.org.

Chapter 4: Lost in Your Father's House

1. Timothy Keller, *The Prodigal God: Recovering the Heart of the Christian Faith* (New York: Dutton/Penguin Group, 2008).
2. Ibid., 37.
3. Ibid., 18.

Chapter 7: Defining God's Glory

1. Fraser Cain, "How Many Stars?" Universe Today website, www.universetoday.com/guide-to-space/stars/how-many-stars.
2. Lisa Lambert, *Exploring Life Science* (New York: Marshall Cavendish, 2006), 88.

Chapter 8: It's All about God's Glory

1. "The World Factbook," Central Intelligence Agency, https://www.cia.gov/library/publications/the-world-factbook/geos/xx.html#Geo.
2. "A Bald Eagle's Eyesight and Hearing," American Bald Eagle Information website, www.baldeagleinfo.com/eagle/eagle2.html.
3. Beth Carter, "Just the Facts: Peregrine Falcon," Field Trip Earth website, North Carolina Zoological Society, www.fieldtripearth.org/article.xml?id=1480.
4. "How High Can a Flea Jump?" Big Site of Amazing Facts website, www.bigsiteofamazingfacts.com/how-high-can-a-flea-jump.
5. Gerald Robison, *Because He Liked It* (Mechanicsville, VA: UnveilinGLORY, 2008).
6. Gerald Robison, *Crocs Eat Rocks* (Mechanicsville, VA: UnveilinGLORY, 2008).
7. We are barely hitting the tip of the iceberg on this topic. A much better theological understanding can be found in chapter 1 of John Piper's book *Desiring God* (Colorado Springs: Multnomah, 2011).

Chapter 12: The Goal of God's Glory

1. John Piper, "We Want You to Be a Christian Hedonist!" http://www.desiringgod.org/resource-library/articles/we-want-you-to-be-a-christian-hedonist.
2. Larry Crabb, *Shattered Dreams: God's Unexpected Pathway to Joy* (Colorado Springs: WaterBrook Press, 2001).
3. John Piper, *God Is the Gospel: Meditations on God's Love as the Gift of Himself* (Wheaton: Crossway), 2005.

Chapter 15: Evangelical Humanists

1. *Dictionary.com Unabridged*, s.v. "humanism," http://dictionary.reference.com/browse/humanism.
2. Free Hugs Campaign, www.freehugscampaign.org.
3. DeVern Fromke, *Unto Full Stature* (Indianapolis: Ministry of Life, 1967).

Chapter 16: A Christian Cancer

1. Joel Osteen, *It's Your Time: Activate Your Faith, Achieve Your Dreams, and Increase in God's Favor* (New York: Free Press, 2009).
2. "Newsroom," October 12, 2009, Persecution.com, The Voice of the Martyrs website, http://www.persecution.com/public/newsroom.aspx?story_ID=MTky.

Chapter 18: Different Levels of Suffering

1. John Foxe, *Foxe's Book of Martyrs* (New Kensington, PA: Whitaker House, 1981).
2. Richard Wurmbrand, "Preparing the Underground Church," *Epiphany Journal* 5, no. 4 (Summer 1985): 46–48.

Chapter 19: The Personal Benefits of Suffering

1. For more on this point, read Bob's book *Unveiled at Last: Discover God's Hidden Message from Genesis to Revelation* (Seattle: YWAM Publishing, 1992).
2. See chapters 4 and 5 of *Unveiled at Last.*

Chapter 20: How Your Suffering Affects Others

1. John Piper, *Let the Nations Be Glad! The Supremacy of God in Missions*, 2nd ed. (Grand Rapids: Baker Academic, 2003), 71.
2. Michael Card, "Wounded in the House of Friends," *Virtue*, March–April 1991, 28–29, 69; quoted in John Piper, *Let the Nations Be Glad! The Supremacy of God in Missions*, 3rd ed. (Grand Rapids: Baker Academic, 2010), 115–16.

Chapter 21: Two Types of Suffering

1. For more information about Keith's ministry, visit www.kw.org.
2. The word used twice in this verse is *raah*, a cognate of *ra*, which has basically the same meaning.

Chapter 22: Ten Reasons Why God Allows Suffering

1. For more on this point, read chapters 6 and 7 of Bob's book *Unveiled at Last: Discover God's Hidden Message from Genesis to Revelation* (Seattle: YWAM Publishing, 1992).

Chapter 23: God's Greatest Glory: Why All Nations?

1. Please note that we are not saying that God can be more glorious because of what we do. He is as glorious as he will ever be. But as the rays of the sun can be diminished by clouds, likewise we can see God's glory better when the "clouds of life" are taken away. This is what we mean

when we talk about bringing God "maximum glory." We want to see his glory at its zenith, and God wants to show it off that way as well.
2. To study this subject in much more depth, see my book *Unveiled at Last: Discover God's Hidden Message from Genesis to Revelation* (Seattle: YWAM Publishing, 1992).

Chapter 24: His Glory: Our Joy!

1. John Piper, "Why God Is Not a Megalomaniac: Encouragement for Pastors" (conference message, College Park Church, Indianapolis, IN, April 27, 2007), audio only available at DesiringGod.org, http://www.desiringgod.org/resource-library/conference-messages/why-god-is-not-a-megalomaniac-encouragement-for-pastors.

Chapter 26: Why the Church?

1. Visit www.perspectives.org to find a class near you.
2. John Piper, *Let the Nations Be Glad! The Supremacy of God in Missions* (Grand Rapids: Baker, 1993), 11.
3. John Foxe, *Foxe's Book of Martyrs* (New Kensington, PA: Whitaker House, 1981).
4. DC Talk and The Voice of the Martyrs, *Jesus Freaks: Stories of Those Who Stood for Jesus: The Ultimate Jesus Freaks* (Tulsa: Albury Publishing, 1999).
5. John Piper, "Doing Missions When Dying Is Gain" (conference message, Wheaton College, Wheaton, IL, October 27, 1996), audio and transcript available at DesiringGod.org, http://www.desiringgod.org/resource-library/conference-messages/doing-missions-when-dying-is-gain.

ALSO AVAILABLE

There is a joke about cats and dogs that conveys their differences perfectly. A dog says, "You pet me, you feed me, you shelter me, you love me; you must be God!" A cat says, "You pet me, you feed me, you shelter me, you love me; I must be God!"

This book challenges the reader's understanding of their relationship with God. Our understanding of how we relate to God may not be wrong, but it may be incomplete. The God-given traits of cats ("you exist to serve me") and dogs ("I exist to serve you") can be similar to certain theological attitudes held by many Christians. In our personal theologies, some attitudes may draw us closer to God, and others can also pull us away from Him. This book will help the reader differentiate those attitudes, and, as a result, draw closer to the God who delights in them!

Paperback, 206 pages, 5.5 x 8.5
ISBN: 978-1-88454-317-3
Retail: $14.99

Available for purchase online or through your local bookstore.

ALSO AVAILABLE

"There is a YOU-shaped hole in God's Kingdom—find it and fill it."
—Patrick Johnstone

How to Be a World-Class Christian reveals God's unfolding drama throughout the world and how you can become part of that story. It will show you how to expand your understanding of God's heart for the nations as it is revealed throughout Scripture. It will increase your global prayer life and align your passions with God's. Using practical tools and observations from everyday life, this book invites each one of us to stretch our knowledge of the purposes of God right at home and throughout the world and then to take the steps necessary to start responding to the opportunities we face. Finding and filling the place in the world that God has designed for you is what *How to Be a World-Class Christian* is designed to do.

In *Purpose-Driven Life*, Rick Warren cites Paul Borthwick's books *A Mind For Missions* and *How to Be a World-Class Christian* as resources that "should be read by every Christian."

Paperback, 237 pages, 5.5 x 8.5
ISBN: 978-1-93406-834-2
Retail: $14.99

Available for purchase online or through your local bookstore.